Enterprise Process Orchestration

A hands-on guide to **strategy**, **people**, and **technology** that will transform your business

Bernd Ruecker and Leon Strauch

Praise by Rob Koplowitz (Former Principal Analyst at Forrester):
If you're serious about the challenges of driving deep and meaningful change through automation in your organization, *Enterprise Process Orchestration* is a must-read. Bernd and Leon tackle the issues head-on with a pragmatic approach to drive success. It's a big job, but your organization's survival might be at stake.

Early access version as of April 26th, 2024
ISBN: 9798882601668

Contents

Preface   **1**
    Notes on EARLY ACCESS 1
    Foreword by Bernd Ruecker 1
    Foreword by Rob Koplowitz (Former Principal Analyst at Forrester and Cofounder of
        Analysis.tech) 4

Introduction   **9**
    Why Change? 9
    The Process Orchestration Adoption Framework 12
    How to Read This Book 16
    Who Should Read This Book 16

Process Orchestration 101   **19**
    Process Orchestration in the Context of Automation 19
        Process Automation = Process Orchestration + Task Automation 20
        Challenges Process Orchestration Solves 21
        Taming Process Complexity 22
        Process Orchestration Engines and Executable Process Models 22
    The Benefits of Process Orchestration 24
        Better Customer Experience 25
        Operational Efficiency 26
        Faster Time to Value and Greater Business Agility 27
        Enabling Artificial Intelligence 29
        Technical Problems Process Orchestration Engines Solve 29
    Understanding Process Types That Can Be Orchestrated 30
        Tailor-Made Digital Processes 31
        Diversity of Business Processes 32
        A Useful Categorization of Use Cases 33
        Tailoring Your Process Automation Approach 34
        Avoiding the Danger Zone Around Vendor Rationalization and Tool Harmonization 35
    Typical Use Cases for Process Orchestration by Industry 36
        Financial Services 36
        Todo: Next Industries… 38

Part 1: Vision   39

    Strategic Alignment: Bridging Vision, Strategy, and Stakeholders 40
        Scoping Your Transformation Journey 40
        Defining Your Vision 41
        Aligning Your Stakeholders 42
    Implementing Change 44
        Understanding Personas 45
        Governing Your Change Process 45
        Why Change Fails and How to Avoid This 47
        The Process-First Mindset 50
    Building Your Transformation Roadmap 50
        Understanding Process Orchestration Work Streams 50
        De-Risking Your Start with Process Tracking 52
        Enterprise Adoption Phases 52
        Prioritization of Use Cases or Domains 54
        Amplifying Organic Bottom-up Initiatives 56
        Finding the Golden Path Between Top-down and Bottom-up Adoption Journeys   58
    Questions to Assess Your Maturity 58

Part II: People   63

    How Software Is Being Built Today 63
        Focused Components That Implement Capabilities 64
        Agile and DevOps 65
        Product Thinking 65
        Process Ownership 66
        Team Topologies 67
        Diversity of Roles 68
        A Healthy Level of Centralization 69
    Delivery Models 71
        Federated Solution Delivery with the CoE as an Accelerator 71
        Fully Decentralized Delivery 73
        Fully Centralized Delivery 75
    Roles 76
        CoE Leader 77
        Enterprise Architect 77
        Rainmaker 78
        Business Analyst 78
        Solution or IT Architect 79
        Software Developer 80
        Low-Code Developer 80
        Operations Engineer 81

- The Center of Excellence (CoE) 82
  - What Is a CoE for Process Orchestration? 82
  - The Scope of Your CoE 82
  - What About Communities of Practice (CoPs)? 83
  - What Should Your CoE Look Like? 84
  - The Business Case for the CoE 86
  - Building Your CoE 88
  - CoE Tasks 89
  - Governance 95
  - Process Architecture and Process Landscapes 96
  - CoE Anti-Patterns 97
  - Real-Life Examples 99
- Defining Your Target Operating Model 100
  - Key Dimensions to Define Your Operating Model 100
  - Sketching Your Journey 103
- Questions to Assess Your Maturity 106

Part III: Technology 109

- Process Orchestration in Your Enterprise Architecture 109
  - Enterprise Architecture: A High-Level View 110
  - Enterprise vs. Solution Scope 112
  - Are Business Processes an Elevated Concept? 114
  - Microservices and Domain-Driven Design 115
  - Agile Approaches Need Architecture Too 117
- Zooming in on the Process Orchestration Capability 118
  - Components Required for Process Orchestration 118
  - Platform Thinking 127
  - Modern Process Orchestration Platforms Don't Become a Bottleneck 130
  - Why Does This Work Now If SOA Failed a Decade Ago? 130
- Operating and Providing a Process Orchestration Platform 132
  - Running a Platform Like Camunda 132
  - Isolation Needs and Multitenancy 134
  - Staging Environments 135
  - Sizing and Scaling 136
  - Resilience and High Availability 136
- Selecting the Right Process Orchestration Technology 137
  - Types of Processes: Standard vs. Tailor-Made 138
  - Scope: Task Automation and Simple Integrations vs. Processes 139
  - Process Complexity: Simple vs. Complex 140
  - Scale: Small vs. Big 141
  - Project Setup: Ad Hoc vs. Strategic 141

    Contrasting Process Orchestration with Adjacent Technologies 142
        Robotic Process Automation (RPA) 142
        Data Flow Engines and Data Streaming 142
        Event-Driven Architecture (EDA) and Event Streaming 143
        BPM Suites and Low-Code Application Platforms 144
        Microservice Orchestrators 144
        Tips on Evaluating Tools 144
    Questions to Assess Your Maturity 147

Part IV: Delivery   **149**
    Solution Creation Approach 149
        Discover 150
        Model 150
        Develop 152
        Run 152
        Monitor 152
    Setting the Stage for Success: Your Early Projects 153
    Typical Delivery Teams and Roles 154
    Solution Design 155
        Greenfield Solution Architecture for Pro-Code Use Cases 156
        The Software Development Lifecycle and Model Roundtrips 157
        Simplified Solution Architecture for Low-Code Use Cases 160
        Typical Questions Around the Development Lifecycle 161
    Accelerating Solution Building 163
    Change Management 164
    Questions to Assess Your Maturity 166

Part V: Measurement   **171**
    Define Metrics and Key Performance Indicators (KPIs) 171
    Evaluate Metrics 171
    Continuously Communicate Value 171
    Questions to Assess Your Maturity 171

Closing Thoughts   **175**
    Continuously Monitor and Improve Your Maturity Level 175
    Further Resources 175
    Where to Get Help 175
    Get Going! 175

References   **177**

Preface

Notes on EARLY ACCESS

The book you hold in your hands is in an "early access" state. That means we're still heavily developing the content. If the book were software, it would be an alpha release.

We're publishing it anyway, for two reasons. First, the content might already be valuable to you—if you're getting started on your own process orchestration endeavor today, a half-baked book that's available now will help you more than a polished one next year. Second, we're really interested in your feedback. The more feedback we get as we discuss the content with many people, both internally and externally to Camunda, the better the result will be.

Also note that different parts of this book are in different maturity stages. For example, the content around centers of excellence (CoEs) is quite mature and has been battle-tested in many customer interactions already. On the other hand, other parts, for example around strategic alignment, still need more work. Our goal with this early access version of the book is to create a skeleton of relevant content on the topic of process orchestration in the enterprise, providing a framework for discussion of questions like "Why is this content important?" and "Why is this missing?"

We hope you treat this early access version accordingly: if you see something that's missing or that you think needs more development, don't be shy or withhold your feedback just because you think we probably know that anyway. You'd be surprised how much gets lost in the book-writing process, when you're trying to squeeze a galaxy of good thoughts into a linear series of characters.

So, happy reading, and let the feedback flow.

- Bernd Ruecker: bernd.ruecker@camunda.com[1]
- Leon Strauch: leon.strauch@camunda.com[2]

Foreword by Bernd Ruecker

In 2008, I co-founded a small boutique consultancy around process automation called Camunda. In 2013, we pivoted from consulting to providing an open source product with the same name.

And around 2018, I learned about a global bank that used Camunda throughout the organization, running millions of process instances per week. But only later did I finally understand more about the secret sauce of applying process orchestration enterprise-wide to achieve great outcomes.

This is what we've distilled into this book.

Five years ago, though, I couldn't have written this book. I was still too naive to understand some core aspects that look obvious to me now, in hindsight (and I hope they'll look obvious to you too, after reading the book). Let me explain.

This book is about adopting process orchestration to automate more, while being faster at it at the same time. It focuses on how to scale the usage across the organization to benefit the company. This is less about the nitty-gritty details of technology and much more about enterprise architecture, staffing teams, getting teams and management on board, getting buy-in, anchoring it in the organization, and a lot of other sociotechnical elements. (Of course, it's also about creating a sound technical solution.)

This book is based on our experiences over the last decade, where we have seen many customers driving Camunda adoption to an impressive scale. Of course, we tried to figure out what differentiated those customers from others that were not as successful. One element crystallized as making a difference: all of those customers had some kind of center of excellence (CoE). Intrigued by this insight, we began to explore CoEs, and as a result a younger me wrote a blog post called "From Project to Program: Establishing a Center of Excellence."[3] In hindsight, this article is a good example of my own naiveness.

Back then, I had a very technical view of things. In the article, I was basically saying that you need to go step by step if you want to end up at a huge scale; you can't just start out at that kind of scale. This had been proven by companies I had seen struggling with platforms where they tried to build too much, too early.

All of this is true, but it misses some important points. This became clear to me when a customer that'd had a Camunda solution in production for multiple years approached me with a problem. To give you the full picture: their project was a success story, the solution ran smoothly, the architecture was beautiful, it had a working CI/CD pipeline, the business understood the Business Process Model and Notation (BPMN) model that helped to drive changes, and our champion was a huge fan that also talked publicly about their success. So, I thought everything was great.

Unfortunately, I was wrong. A newer project in the company was also using process orchestration. But, for unknown reasons, they didn't even talk to our champion before getting started, even though he was well connected in the enterprise. And they chose a different tool—a competitor of ours. When we dug into it, we could see that there were no solid reasons for this decision. It seemed that the team simply wanted to demonstrate their autonomy to make their own decisions. A bit later, upper management started to question the use of two different tools to solve the same problem, as they (as organizations commonly do) began looking into vendor rationalization and tool harmonization. And rightfully so—there is typically no good reason to have two different solutions solving exactly the same problem! Frustratingly, in this case the competitor ended up in pole position, as the newer tool was considered more modern—which is a hundred percent not true if you look at how Camunda has reinvented itself a couple of times in the past.

The sad thing about this anecdote is that it's also a bad situation for the customer organization. They need to invest effort in tool selection twice and get to grips with two different tools; the teams can't learn from each other's mistakes, and investment may be needed to migrate one of the tools later. At the same time, there will be political games at play, and the fans of the different tools may start to fight each other. Of course, there's always room for healthy competition as tools age or disruptive ideas come along (in fact, a good chunk of Camunda's success was down to eating into the business of aging tools from companies like IBM or Pega)—but that wasn't the case here.

So, I dug further to better understand the situation. And what I came up with was a simple conclusion: it's not enough to create an awesome solution locally in a bigger organization. A great solution is necessary, but not sufficient. You also have to think about a lot of other aspects.

Like: What's the business value of the solution? What is Camunda's contribution? How do you make sure process orchestration gets the right visibility throughout the organization? What governance should be established, and how do you make sure there's a healthy level of standardization on tools? How can you help other teams adopt Camunda? How does this all align with the vision of the organization? Who might champion Camunda higher up in the hierarchy? How do the business departments understand what Camunda does? Who can (internally) help to differentiate between process orchestration and robotic process automation?

Quite importantly, you also need to form a bigger vision. This is the piece I missed in the above-mentioned blog post. So, even if you don't start with a company-wide program, you need to know where you want to end up, get buy-in for this strategically, and then of course come down to earth again to start the first project. We see this type of adoption journey, which has clear top management commitment, as being much more successful when applied in our customers' organizations.

Don't get me wrong: this is not me trying to get as many dollars out of organizations as possible. It's about applying the right technology in the right way to benefit from it properly and to harvest the competitive advantage process orchestration can bring to the table.

So, we came to realize that we need to help our customers do the right thing, or at least put the right things they are already doing into perspective in the organization. And that's why I wanted to write this book. While it will talk about strategy, we've made sure it is always rooted in concrete experience and technology solutions that we have seen working in real life.

Luckily, I found a great partner in crime for the writing journey. Leon had worked in Camunda's customer success department and interacted with a lot of our client organizations on their every-day problems. He recently switched to a role that manages the process orchestration adoption framework we will introduce in this book. He is hungry for improvement, very structured, and quite strategic.

These are already too many words for a foreword, but I hope it helps you understand what this book is all about and why it's important to read it. I am happy beyond words that you can hold this early access copy in your hands now. As it's an early access version, it is far from being finished, but we wanted to get it out as soon as possible so readers can start deriving value from it—and of course, to collect as much feedback as possible to improve the draft while working toward the final book.

With that in mind, I hope you'll enjoy the book, whether you read it cover to cover or cherry-pick the topics that are relevant to you today. And more importantly, I hope you'll also enjoy applying process orchestration—that's what I do every day!

Bernd Ruecker

March 2024

PS: If you just won a bullshit bingo during the foreword alone, don't worry! We'll cut through the marketing fluff so that you can understand what all this is really about, and how you can make the best out of it.

PPS: I also need to thank countless people who helped make this happen. Naming any of them would force me to draw a line between who to name and who not to, so I decided not to name any of them personally—but I still want to thank them. First, I'd like to thank each and every one of my fellow Camundis: you are such great folks, and without you neither Camunda nor this book would have ever been possible. The same goes for our great customers: you do amazing things with process orchestration, and I am beyond happy that you've decided to share your experiences with us. Last but not least, a big thank you to all our partners, who bring decades of experience around process automation to the table. Thank you all!

Foreword by Rob Koplowitz (Former Principal Analyst at Forrester and Cofounder of Analysis.tech)

Organizations face an automation imperative, and for many, it will be crucial to their survival. Automation at scale is no longer about driving efficiency or cutting costs; it's focused on building a foundation for business agility and innovation. As an industry analyst, I've spent the last decade tracking the market's interest in core automation topics like BPMN. I watched as interest in these topics waned until roughly eight years ago. Then, trends shifted dramatically. What happened?

Organizations began to get serious about the need for broad-scale automation. We saw an increasing number of strategies coalesce around a very critical concept: orchestration. And one vendor became central to the trend—Camunda. So, when Bernd approached me to write a forward for their book *Enterprise Process Orchestration*, my first thought was "Ooh, early access!"

I cracked open the book, and by the next day I had read it cover to cover. Our firm, Analysis.tech, was founded to address the reality that most automation initiatives currently fall short of driving true transformation. *Enterprise Process Orchestration* tackles this challenge head-on. I often use the analogy that huge automation projects are like turning an aircraft carrier, as they require massive budgets and resources. Make no mistake, most of these initiatives have been worth it; however, transforming your organization so it has a true process and automation mindset is like turning 5,000 speedboats in unison.

The central theme of this book is orchestration. From a business perspective, a focus on orchestration provides a context for breaking through silos created by legacy systems and organizational boundaries and driving true transformation at scale. This is where tomorrow's innovation and disruption will come from—but it's hard to get there.

What I truly appreciate about Bernd and Leon's approach to this crucial topic is the pragmatic advice backed by real-world examples and strong technical underpinnings. It requires careful thought and planning to drive organizational change. It also requires a well-thought-out technical architecture. In *Enterprise Process Orchestration*, Bernd and Leon offer a detailed approach to technology selection, maturity models, and governance, and a guide to help your organization build a process-first mindset. I was particularly excited about the section that defined the different models for a center of excellence, a critical part of a successful process automation strategy.

If you're serious about the challenges of driving deep and meaningful change through automation in your organization, *Enterprise Process Orchestration* is a must-read. Bernd and Leon tackle the issues head-on with a pragmatic approach to drive success. It's a big job, but your organization's survival might be at stake.

Introduction

In 2024, Forrester[4] reported that TK, a big German health insurance company, had reduced the happy path for its denture reimbursement process from about 1.5 weeks to 2.7 seconds through process automation and digital data exchange with dentists. This is a great example of hitting two targets with one arrow: not only did they lower operational costs through process automation, but they also hugely improved the customer experience. What's more, the newly orchestrated processes can be infused with innovative technologies like AI to drive further improvements.

This is not an isolated success story, but part of a wider shift in how business value is created: according to Camunda's State of Process Orchestration 2024 report[5], 91% of companies surveyed have seen increased business growth due to process automation within the last year. In addition, 95% say automation has helped them achieve operational efficiency, and 93% say automation has helped improve customer experiences. In that sense, process automation has become table stakes for organizations to remain competitive.

At the same time, according to the report, just 50% of organizational processes have been automated so far, many of those in a scrappy fashion. In that sense, there is a huge opportunity to improve the customer and employee experience, while becoming more agile and efficient. The downside is that you cannot rest—if your organization doesn't do this successfully, someone else will, and will possibly outcompete you.

Why Change?

A while ago, one of our customers, a top 10 insurance company in Germany, was startled by the results of its latest customer survey. The company found that customer satisfaction with the speed of claim processing had declined dramatically over the last three years (Figure 1). However, digging deeper into their performance, they found that the process time had remained stable over that period. So why had customer satisfaction gone down? The most likely explanation: customer expectations have shifted massively. We've all gotten used to the lightning speed of the digital economy on our smartphones. Have groceries delivered to your home in a few minutes? No problem. Instantly open a bank account online? Done. Get a new eSIM in a matter of seconds? Easy. Wait 10 days for your insurance claim to be processed? No thank you!

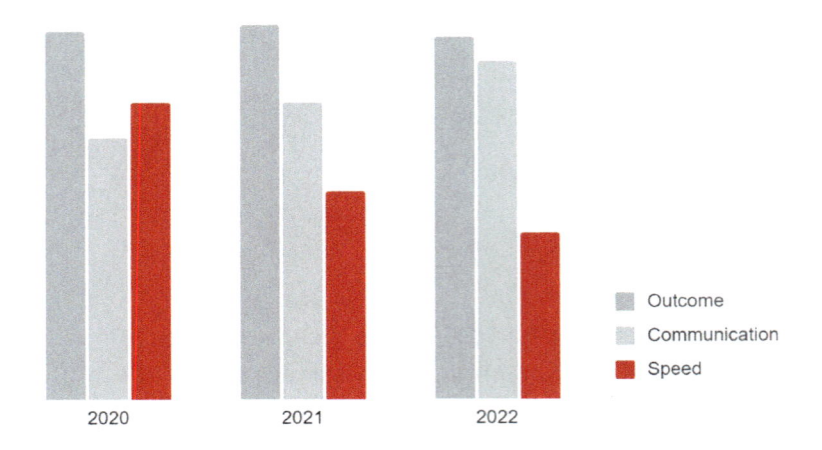

Figure 1: Customer satisfaction with outcomes, communication, and speed

This story of declining customer satisfaction is the reality in almost any business domain, and digitally minded organizations are beginning to eat up incumbent market share by providing a superior customer experience with high operational efficiency.

For example, a recent study around the Know Your Customer (KYC) checks[6] that banks need to do when onboarding new corporate clients found that 48% of banks lost clients because of slow and inefficient onboarding, and four out of five of those banks attribute that loss to delayed processing. To give you an idea of what "delayed" means, banks took on average 95 days to complete a KYC review in 2023. That's more than three months! And this finding needs to be viewed against the background that customers have more choices by the day, be it via FinTechs or BigTechs like Amazon Finance for Business. Those new players are disrupting with speed and agility. This has led to more and more traditional banks partnering with these players (for example, using Plaid for eKYC). But is your company ready to make such fundamental process changes?

At the same time, we are at the end of a decade-long period of virtually free money through near-zero interest rates. We're currently seeing a profound, global macroeconomic shift, with interest rates unlikely to return to pre-Covid levels. Accordingly, organizations will have to hone in on efficiency and achieve more with less.

The same goes for the looming threat of demographic change: as the US Bureau of Labor Statistics[7] points out, the size of the workforce in the United States will continue to decline over the next decade—and this amidst an already existing shortage of skilled workers. The situation is the same in the European Union and especially in Germany, where The Economist[8] reported in 2022 that almost 50% of companies said that they were unable to secure enough skilled workers (with the public sector being especially battered by this trend).

And it's not only market pressure that organizations are facing today. The ever-growing regulatory pressure is another hurdle, especially in the finance industry. In May 2024, the US security settlements cycle will be reduced to what is known as "T+1," which essentially means that a trade needs to be settled within 24 hours. Before that change, the cycle was two days. This is a huge challenge for banks. According to BNP Paribas[9], "The execution through settlement phases will need to be automated and modernized to enhance straight-through processing and minimize exceptions. While that will take investment, it will strip out manual workflows and bring operating efficiencies, cost savings and risk reduction." But at the time of writing, most banks are struggling to achieve T+1 through process automation. Until they do, they will need to do what is known as "throwing people at the problem," meaning they'll need to rely on an increasing number of people working on trade settlements under extreme time pressure. This is expensive and harms the employee experience; it is thus not sustainable and ultimately risky. Such regulatory pressure is not only evident in the finance industry, but among other verticals too; just think of healthcare, pharmaceuticals, telecommunications, utilities, and other areas where stringent regulations shape operations and compliance is paramount.

Increasing customer expectations, cost pressure, demographic change, a growing regulatory regime, and more—how are organizations supposed to react to this? The intuitive answer is by leveraging technology to drive innovation, automate more, and optimize processes. But isn't this what most organizations have been already doing for a while now?

Well, yes and no. When it comes to process automation, we have seen plenty of organizations driving improvements locally. For example, you might have used robotic process automation (RPA) to automate the data entry in one of your core systems, or implemented a chatbot to automatically answer simple customer questions, or installed a new AI-fueled system for fraud detection.

Many of those initiatives doubtless generated initial business value and yielded local improvements. The challenge is that those are isolated projects and point solutions. Accordingly, they do not create an ecosystem within which an organization can improve its end-to-end customer journey. In fact, the data suggests exactly the opposite: as more and more tasks get automated locally, the overall end-to-end process becomes more difficult to maintain due to the increasing complexity of the IT landscape (so say 68% of IT decision makers in our State of Process Orchestration 2024 report[10]). Point solutions tend to be brittle and hard to maintain, and due to their local nature are often not embedded in a global corporate strategy.

This leads to a value trap for process automation. By automating locally, your organization compounds technical and organizational debt that undermines the initially achieved value. Managing all those point solutions effectively makes it harder to control the core business processes, leading to reduced flexibility, longer time to market, and a lack of business visibility.

This loss of process control hampers the ability to adapt or innovate, as you end up getting bogged down with maintaining your spaghetti integrations and legacy systems. This unfortunate situation nurtures the cliché of IT as a bottleneck for innovation instead of a business enabler, and widens the gap between business and IT.

So what to do? One of our customers recently described it very well: "We have our systems, and somehow everything works, but it's very hard to change anything. What we need to do is think more in terms of processes."

This is where enterprise process orchestration comes into play. We have seen an increasing number of organizations successfully escape that value trap by orchestrating customer journeys end-to-end, which means that you will not rip your IT landscape apart but seamlessly integrate all the existing systems along the process chain, using graphical models that can be directly executed by process orchestration platforms.

This allows you to tame the complexity of integrating your existing systems and focus on generating business value. Process orchestration brings together business and IT, as process models provide a common view and thus transparency on value streams. It also increases your organization's agility and improves time to value for future initiatives, as various stakeholders are able to understand the processes and join the discussion. All of this brings you to a state where you are able to automate more processes and adapt to changes faster, while bringing down technical debt.

Sounds good? Yes, indeed. Let's explore how to get there.

The Process Orchestration Adoption Framework

In contrast to siloed integrations, enterprise process orchestration is, as the name suggests, applied globally across an organization. This means that you need to involve a lot of people throughout the whole enterprise to drive the change you want to make, from top management to subject matter experts to software developers.

To help our customers with that, we have developed the process orchestration adoption framework. This framework can help you to transform your business by aiming for a strategic, scaled adoption of process orchestration. It provides guidance on all the steps of an iterative and agile journey that you can follow to generate value incrementally and learn fast.

The framework defines various maturity stages your company can be in, and it calls out the five drivers that are most important to look at when you want to define your current maturity and derive a roadmap from this. The five drivers, as visualized in Figure 2, are:

- **Vision:** Are people aware what process orchestration is and why it is valuable to the organization? Is there awareness of typical use cases? Why does enterprise process orchestration matter to the organization? What goals is the organization trying to achieve through its process orchestration practice?
- **People:** What people and skills do you need? How can you set up the right team structures? Who will define the standards and policies for how process orchestration should be used? Who is responsible for driving the change? What does the operating model look like? Are the right people empowered and enabled to do the right things?

- **Technology:** What technology philosophies, platforms, and solutions power the organization's process orchestration efforts? How does this fit into your overall enterprise architecture?
- **Delivery:** How are concrete process automation solutions being developed and deployed?
- **Measurement:** How does the organization define process orchestration success, and how capably can the organization track that success?

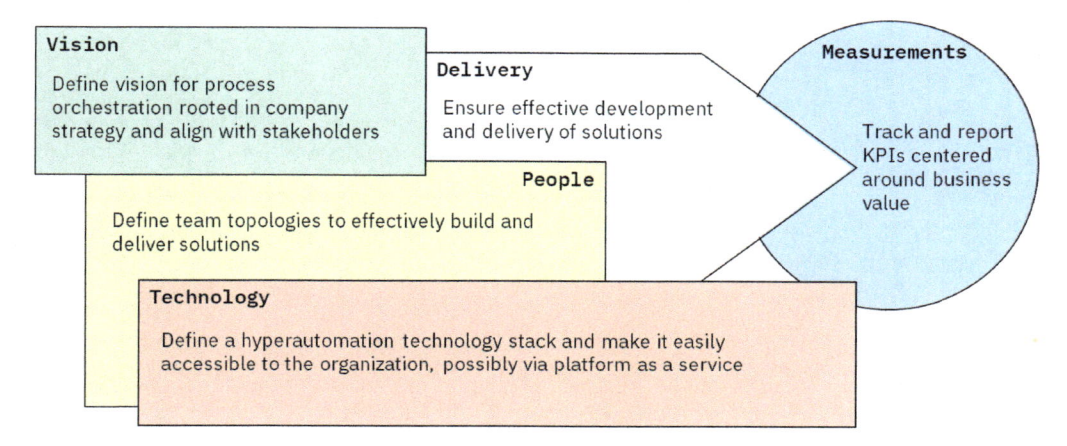

Vision
Define vision for process orchestration rooted in company strategy and align with stakeholders

Delivery
Ensure effective development and delivery of solutions

Measurements
Track and report KPIs centered around business value

People
Define team topologies to effectively build and deliver solutions

Technology
Define a hyperautomation technology stack and make it easily accessible to the organization, possibly via platform as a service

Figure 2: The five key drivers of process orchestration maturity

You can rate your own organization's maturity for each of these drivers individually, on a scale from 1 (undeveloped) to 5 (excellent). Doing so not only helps you understand your strengths better, but also your gaps. This allows you to develop an enterprise strategy and roadmap to build the required capabilities to succeed with enterprise process orchestration.

Figure 3 lists the different levels of maturity for each of these drivers as we have experienced them through our customer engagements.

	Level 1: Undeveloped	Level 2: Basic	Level 3: Competent	Level 4: Advanced	Level 5: Excellent
Vision	Processes are not working efficiently or effectively. Some process tasks may have automated components, but those tasks are too dispersed for the effects of automation to be measured.	Focused on single, mission-critical process orchestration projects, or projects that center around a "broken" process.	Broader, scaled-up initiatives are focused on better business outcomes; measuring success remains a challenge.	Evolving toward a practice where process orchestration supports organization-wide digital transformation goals. This allows harnessing process orchestration to drive strategic business outcomes, at scale and at a rapid pace, for the entire organization.	There's a clearly defined strategy around technology, methodology, and people to execute process orchestration at scale, matched by the ability to execute that vision. A demonstrated track record of delivering strategic value to the organization through process orchestration motivates teams to deliver business transformation at scale.
People	IT team is not set up to centralize projects or resources.	Disparate process orchestration projects are implemented in a decentralized manner (the "sprouting mushrooms" approach).	Team seeks to empower business roles to understand their process orchestration projects.	A center of excellence (CoE) or distributed team focused on repeatability, enablement, and scale has been established.	A global CoE acts as a SaaS platform within the organization, providing enablement, training, and internal consulting and developing connectors for process orchestration technology solutions.
Technology	Teams may have implemented disparate automation technologies.	Teams are questioning the continued use of legacy systems or monolithic on-premise solutions that limit advancement.	The focus is on building a single technology stack that covers the entire process lifecycle.	Investing in elements that increase solution acceleration, with a focus on enabling multiple teams to build process orchestration solutions at scale.	Recognizing that there is no "one-size-fits-all" approach to hyperautomated tech stacks, the organization has instead built one that fits its exact needs; it also has a dedicated process orchestration strategy within the stack.
Delivery	Large gaps between business and IT create silos, leading to slow iterations and limited ability to deliver impactful process solutions.	Business starts to recognize the transformational potential of IT, but lack of mature IT methodologies prevents agile delivery in small increments.	As business and IT alignment improves and the organization shifts to more agile development, teams begin to deliver continuous improvements in short sprints based on process data.	Multiple BizDevOps teams are involved in delivery and establishing best practices that speed up time to value; improved process monitoring allows organizations to track impact on business outcomes.	Business teams can self-serve on an increasing number of use cases with minimal IT involvement, enabled by the CoE; processes are purpose-built to drive business value and adjusted through continuous monitoring and improvement to maximize value.
Measurement	Unable to accurately measure business value due to silos and lack of scale.	Teams are focused on completing single high-need projects; success is defined as "project is in production."	The focus is on defining and measuring success for individual projects and/or processes. Tracking key performance indicators (KPIs) is still a struggle.	Clear success metrics have been established for individual process orchestration projects; starting to explore broader process orchestration KPIs.	The focus is on defining and measuring large-scale KPIs that demonstrate process orchestration's contribution to business outcomes.

Figure 3: The five maturity levels, across each key driver

Figure 4 shows an example of what your maturity assessment might look like when you have started to apply process orchestration in a handful of first projects driven by IT (a situation we often see with our customers). You have some strength around process orchestration technology and solution delivery, but you need to evolve your vision, establish scalable structures in your teams, and improve at measuring success.

Figure 4: An example maturity assessment for a company getting started on its process orchestration journey

The process orchestration adoption framework, and hence this book, provides concrete hands-on guidance on how to increase maturity in all of those drivers.

In addition to the individual drivers discussed above, we also rate the overall degree of process orchestration adoption in the enterprise along five levels, which again will help you get an idea of where you stand and communicate the status quo alongside the target state internally:

- **Level 0—No process orchestration:** No process orchestration solutions
- **Level 1—Single project:** Adoption in a single project or team, maybe as a proof of concept
- **Level 2—Broader initiative:** Multiple initiatives in one domain (e.g., the health insurance department in an insurance company may be orchestrating multiple processes)
- **Level 3—Distributed adoption:** Multiple domains, with multiple initiatives (e.g., the health insurance and also life and composite insurance departments are strategically using process orchestration)
- **Level 4—Strategic, scaled adoption:** Multiple end-to-end customer journeys across domains, automated intentionally through a holistic enterprise strategy

We discuss the drivers and adoption levels further on our website, where we introduce the Process Orchestration Maturity Model[11].

The process orchestration adoption framework serves as a holistic methodology that organizations can use to drive their process orchestration maturity. We derived this framework by speaking to hundreds of our global customers about their successes and failures, best practices, and lessons learned—and we've distilled that knowledge into this book.

How to Read This Book

The drivers described in the previous section form the five main pillars (or chapters) of this book: vision, people, technology, delivery, and measurement. We have planned the book so that you can read it cover to cover, but you can also start with the section that is most important to you at the moment.

In "Process Orchestration 101" starting on page 19, we will explain the basics of process orchestration and the business value you can achieve by adopting it. Understanding this is crucial to building a vision to get both IT and business stakeholders onboard for your initiative. Building that vision is the focus of "Part 1: Vision" starting on page 39. In that chapter, we will also discuss how you can align your stakeholders, set up proper governance to implement the changes associated with process orchestration, and develop an adoption roadmap.

"Part II: People" starting on page 63 is all about people and team structures. We will look at how software is being built today, and how this will affect your process orchestration initiative. We'll also explore the delivery models organizations can choose to realize these initiatives, and which roles need to be involved. Then, we will discuss a concept that's key to successful adoption: how to set up the right operating model for your center of excellence to support your goals and company culture.

Getting the technology right is, of course, equally important. In "Part III: Technology" starting on page 109, we will focus on the process orchestration tech stack and (enterprise) architecture. We will look at the components you will need, the accelerators you can build, and how to operate and run an internal platform.

In "Part IV: Delivery" starting on page 149, we will explore best practices for successfully delivering solutions across all the project stages, from modeling a process to implementing typical solution architectures.

Once you have your solutions in place, you will need to continuously measure and monitor the value you are achieving with those solutions. In "Part V: Measurement" starting on page 171, we will look at ways you can do that successfully, in order to sustain your gains and get further buy-in.

One last note: as we pointed out at the outset, *this is the early access version and a first MVP*. Not every section is fully developed yet. We will thoroughly edit and expand the book based on further learnings and the feedback we receive—and we hope you'll contribute by sharing your feedback with us, once you've read the book!

Who Should Read This Book

We wrote this book as a practical guide for every persona involved in your process orchestration initiative—all the way from the C-suite to the operational level.

Those who are driving initiatives holistically, especially IT leaders, CoE leaders, and enterprise and IT architects, will benefit from reading the book cover to cover. If you are one of those leaders, ideally you will then pass it around, pointing others to specific parts that are relevant to their roles. This can help you get stakeholders on board with process orchestration across your organization. For example, business leaders who you want to get interested in process orchestration should at least read through "Process Orchestration 101" starting on page 19.

Many roles can benefit from the information in this book. Here are a few pointers:

- **C-suite executives** (especially CIOs) that want to transform their business with process orchestration should read "Process Orchestration 101" starting on page 19 and "Part 1: Vision" starting on page 39, as they are most often responsible for kicking off the necessary changes and getting relevant stakeholders on board (the CEO, CFO, IT leaders, and different business domains). CIOs should also read about team structures, mapped out in "Part II: People" starting on page 63, as well as the technological underpinnings discussed at the beginning of "Part III: Technology" starting on page 109.
- **CoE leaders** can read this book from start to finish to learn how to drive enterprise adoption of process orchestration.
- **IT leaders** that are enabling process orchestration initiatives should mostly focus on "Process Orchestration 101" starting on page 19, "Part II: People" starting on page 63, "Part III: Technology" starting on page 109, and "Part IV: Delivery" starting on page 149. But typically, it makes sense to also look at "Part 1: Vision" starting on page 39.
- **Business leaders** should read "Process Orchestration 101" starting on page 19 to identify use cases for their lines of business.
- **Business and enterprise architects** who are playing a key role in the process orchestration initiative should read the book in full, as they are instrumental in unifying all parts of the business around a shared process orchestration vision.
- **Developers** will benefit from reading "Part III: Technology" starting on page 109 and "Part IV: Delivery" starting on page 149 to understand the technology behind process orchestration and how solutions are built. They should also at least skim through "Process Orchestration 101" starting on page 19 and "Part 1: Vision" starting on page 39.
- **Business analysts** will benefit from the overview of the project lifecycle in "Part IV: Delivery" starting on page 149. This will help them understand their contributions in context. "Part V: Measurement" starting on page 171 is also important to understand how to measure performance and business impact, and we recommend reading "Process Orchestration 101" starting on page 19 as well.

Of course, there are even more personas that can benefit from this book. If we didn't mention your specific role, please don't put it down just yet—skim through, read the parts that are of interest to you, and let us know if you think we should call out your role explicitly in the list above.

We wish you happy reading, and great success with your transformation initiatives!

Process Orchestration 101

First things first: in this chapter we'll dive into what process orchestration is, explore how it differs from process automation, and make a compelling business case for using it. As you'll see, there are very different types of processes that you can automate, and this influences how you build solutions in a big way. While this is not surprising at all, it is surprisingly often ignored in real life.

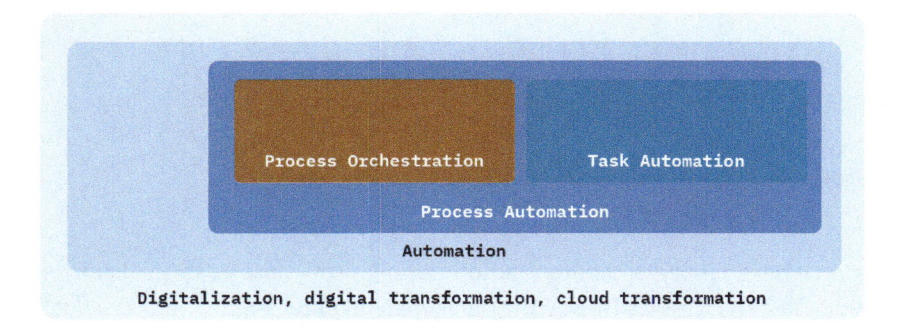

Process Orchestration in the Context of Automation

Automation is a big field. This book concentrates specifically on the automation of processes, and even more specifically on the (automated) orchestration of tasks (rather than on the automation of the tasks themselves). Figure 5 visualizes this relationship. As the distinction can be a little confusing, we'll emphasize it once more—while process automation and task automation are closely related to process orchestration, they are not the same:

- **Task automation** is the use of technology to automatically perform certain tasks without human intervention.
- **Process orchestration** is the coordination of the different tasks of a process, both automated and manual.
- **Process automation** is a mix of process orchestration and task automation to automate a process, where the degree of automation can vary.

Figure 5: Process orchestration in the context of automation

Process orchestration is often compared to the role of a conductor in an orchestra, who makes sure everyone performs at the right time—they tell the musicians when each instrument needs to play to ensure that the song sounds as it should. The process orchestrator is the "conductor" of a process, coordinating and managing the interactions and dependencies of all the tasks in the process, be they human or automated. You can very well orchestrate a process comprising only human tasks.

Process Automation = Process Orchestration + Task Automation

Let's dive a little more deeply into this. Successful automation of (end-to-end) processes includes two distinct ingredients:

- **Task automation** focuses on automating individual tasks. This is often also referred to as *local automation*. For example, in a bank account opening process, the credit scoring of the applicant might be done by an RPA bot instead of manually by a clerk. Or, even better, an API might be used to do the scoring automatically.

- **Process orchestration** coordinates the tasks of an end-to-end process throughout the process flow, maintaining a constant awareness of the status of each instance and what happens next. This includes automated tasks (e.g., via APIs) and manual tasks (e.g., handled by clerks) in a central task list. Using process orchestration allows the gradual automation of human tasks, using RPA or fully API-driven automations. It also provides the basis to inject AI into processes.

The two concepts are orthogonal to each other, as illustrated in Figure 6.

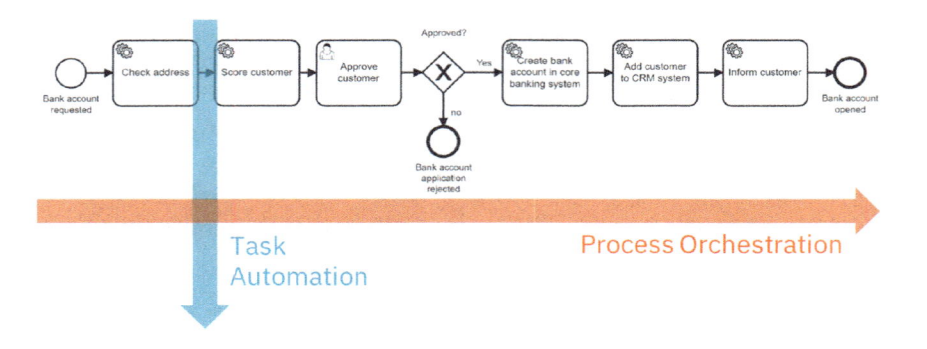

Figure 6: An example bank account opening process

Depending on where you start, different automation journeys are possible. Let's look at a few scenarios, knowing that the reality might be anywhere in between:

1. **You start with process orchestration, and automate tasks later.** You could capture a completely manual process in a process model, orchestrating only human tasks. The

automated process controlled by an orchestrator will replace sending emails, for example, with a task list, thereby standardizing the business process and improving time to resolution and the quality of results. This allows you to make sure that processes are finished as intended and SLAs are hit. It also allows you to analyze cycle times and uncover bottlenecks in your processes.

This is a good starting point to incrementally automate discrete tasks within a process, step by step, with the priority driven by the value of task automation. For example, in our bank account opening process you might want to automate the address check first, as this is both simple to do and a monotonous and error-prone task when performed by humans.

This journey involves a lot of change management to get your people on board.

2. **You started with task automation, and now you need to add process orchestration**. Many organizations run local automation projects, for example to automate an address check or grab an order from a CSV file in some email inbox. Sometimes, RPA is used for those projects. While the automations have a local return on investment (ROI) they don't necessarily improve the overall end-to-end process, as process instances might still go south between those local automations. So, you introduce process orchestration to coordinate the existing local automations.

   This requires removing any direct integrations between the local task automations, so that the orchestrator can take over. An interesting technique to de-risk this transition is to use process tracking, as described in "De-Risking Your Start with Process Tracking" starting on page 52.

In summary, you might be starting with process orchestration of human tasks and looking to automate tasks later on a step-by-step basis, or you might already have discrete or locally automated tasks that you need to roll up into seamlessly automated end-to-end processes. Regardless, *for successful process automation you need both process orchestration and task automation*.

Note that we will speak of "endpoints" when we refer to what process orchestration orchestrates. Those endpoints can be systems and APIs, devices or bots, or, of course, humans.

Challenges Process Orchestration Solves

Process orchestration coordinates many different process endpoints and can tie multiple processes together, for example to orchestrate end-to-end customer journeys.

Without process orchestration, you have a disconnected set of local tasks and (potentially) automations, which leads to challenges such as:

- **Lack of understanding:** The end-to-end process is not fully visible, and key metrics are hard to track.
- **Lack of flexibility:** Changing the end-to-end process is difficult, since it will likely lead to changes in many different systems.
- **Lack of standardization:** Silos in business and IT, as well as point integrations, prevent standardization and thus hamper business and IT collaboration.
- **Broken end-to-end automation:** Since local automations are not integrated with one another, the end-to-end process is not fully automated.

Process orchestration software then has to solve the following challenges:

- **Endpoint diversity:** Processes span across a number of possible process endpoints. The software must be able to easily orchestrate all of those, including a diverse set of technical protocols as well as humans (via graphical user interfaces or chat-like communication).
- **Process complexity:** End-to-end processes are typically more than just simple sequences of steps, so your process orchestration software needs to be able to execute complex flow logic, such as, for instance, exceptions, parallel processing, and loops, for those orchestrations. A powerful modeling language like Business Process Model and Notation (BPMN) is key to achieving this.

Finally, a process orchestration solution needs to:

- **Bring business and IT together:** To automate business processes, you need to involve many stakeholders from all parts of your organization. You will need a common language to talk about processes.
- **Promote innovation:** Process orchestration promotes innovation by connecting business and technology silos faster, more smoothly, and at a lower total cost.
- **Operate at scale:** Of course, the chosen technical solution needs to run at the scale you require for your business. Fortunately, most modern process orchestration platforms can run at any scale, so for example, at Camunda we have large banks running payment flows via the orchestration platform without issues.

Taming Process Complexity

TODO

Process Orchestration Engines and Executable Process Models

To get everybody on the same page, let's take a very quick look into how process orchestration really works (without going into too much technical detail).

To orchestrate a process, you start by defining a blueprint of it, called the *process definition*. This is a model typically expressed in BPMN, the ISO standard for modeling processes graphically, that is then directly executable. Figure 7 shows an example.

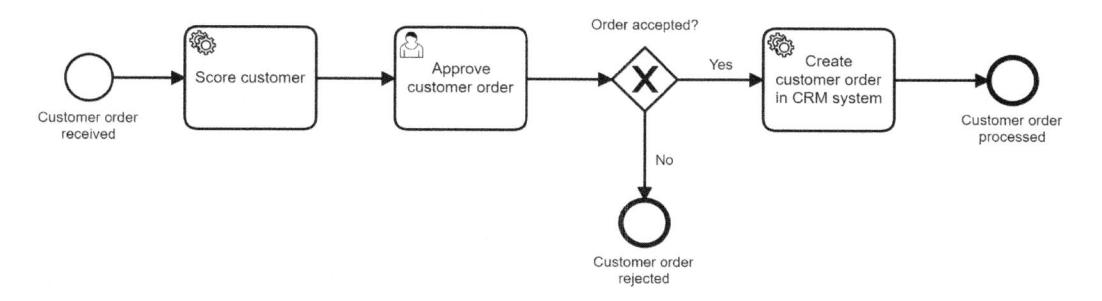

Figure 7: An onboarding process described in BPMN

The model defines where the process starts and ends, including all tasks along the way and the relationships between them. It can also have decision points where the flow goes one way or another. We won't explain BPMN in detail in this book, but it can execute the very advanced patterns required to automate the complexity of everyday processes very well. For more information, we recommend taking a look at *Real-Life BPMN*[12], by Jakob Freund and Bernd Ruecker.

Behind the graphical part, the process model contains various technical attributes that are needed to execute the process definition on an orchestration engine—for example, the exact logic to really make the decision if an order is accepted, the glue code or connector configuration for integrating the scoring system, or forms for the human interaction around approval.

The orchestration engine, often also referred to as a *workflow engine*, now automates the control of process instances. For example, it starts process instances upon receipt of new customer orders, and it keeps track of their state throughout their entire lifetime.

Here are a few key points to keep in mind:

- Process orchestration does not necessarily mean that the entire process is fully automated. What is automated is the *coordination* of the process.
- The central component is the orchestration engine, which executes an executable process model.
- The orchestration engine controls the process by informing humans of tasks that they need to do, and it handles the result of what those people did. This can be done, for example, through user interfaces like task lists or by leveraging chat infrastructure.
- The orchestration engine also communicates with internal and external IT systems.
- The orchestration engine decides which tasks or service calls take place and under what conditions, based on the results of previous tasks and service calls. Thus, the people involved still can influence the operational sequence of an automated process via data.

- Processes can be long-running in nature, meaning they can run for minutes or for hours, days, weeks, or even months.

We typically illustrate what an orchestration engine does with a screenshot of the graphical tooling that comes with it. In Figure 8 you can see an overview page of Camunda's operations tool, showing some technical incidents for the customer scoring, and process instances waiting for approval.

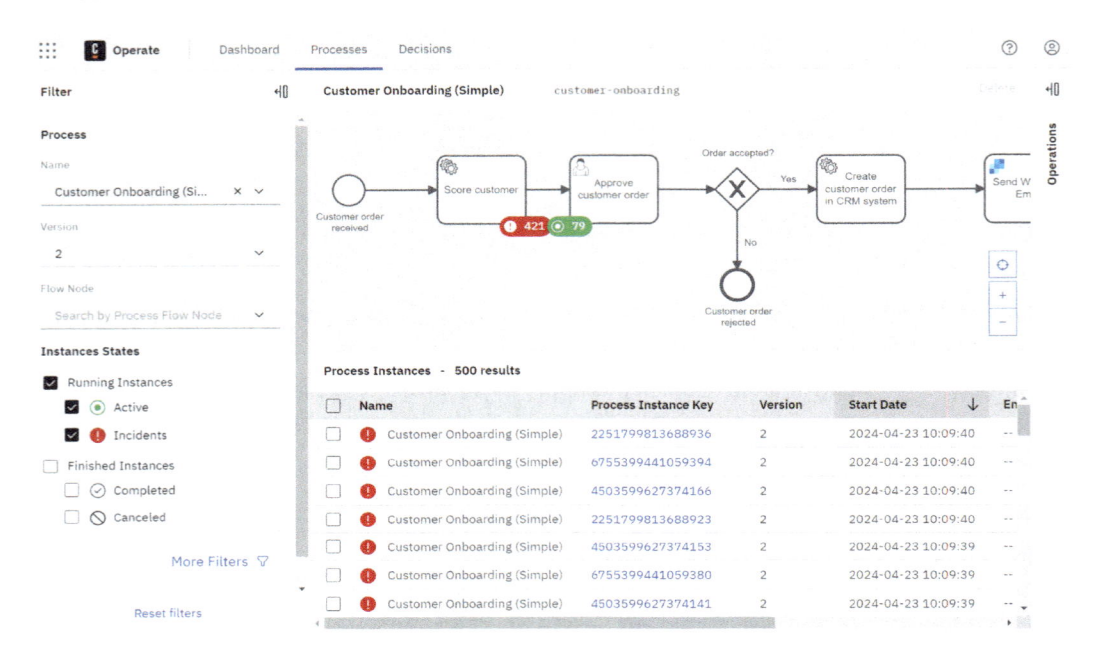

Figure 8: Camunda Operate

The Benefits of Process Orchestration

In early 2024, the research firm Forrester conducted a Total Economic Impact™ (TEI) study for Camunda. As part of this study, Forrester interviewed customers that had been using the Camunda platform for a while to quantify the achieved return on investment. Their key finding was that "Strategic, scaled investments in process automation with Camunda can: 1) improve customer experiences, 2) increase employee productivity, 3) enhance business agility, and 4) reduce business risks. Leaders who center process orchestration within their businesses do more than increase efficiencies—they transform their organizations."

Forrester also put this finding in concrete numbers for a composite organization that it created based on the learnings: the organization achieved a total ROI of 410%, which translated to $116.11 million! You can find more information on this quite impressive number in the TEI study from Forrester[13].

So, there's definitely a huge opportunity here. Let's dive a bit deeper into the business value that process orchestration offers, so that you can understand how those numbers came about and, in turn, create more tangible business cases that are tied to your own corporate strategy. We believe it's crucial to lay this out in detail, as we have seen so many organizations struggling to qualify and quantify the potential business impact.

Better Customer Experience

As discussed in this book's introduction, today's customers expect:

- Immediate processing of their requests (e.g., purchasing a new mobile data plan)
- Self-service options (e.g., a public services portal for community citizens)
- Transparency on the current status of request processing (e.g., updates on insurance damage claim settlements)

To achieve all of that, organizations need to automate (customer-facing) value chains to orchestrate the customer journey in an optimal way. This is obviously not a trivial task. For example, most organizations need to satisfy omnichannel requirements, as different customers might expect them to be available via their preferred channel (website, chatbot, email, messenger, etc.). Technologies and customer expectations in this area are evolving rapidly, and organizations need to keep up to maintain their market share (or better, move fast to gain market share).

At the same time, most businesses—especially large incumbent organizations—have core business capabilities in existing legacy systems of record, like a core banking system, customer relationship management (CRM) system, or enterprise resource planning (ERP) system. Those systems are typically slow-moving and stable; they don't have a lot of changing requirements on a daily basis. They are also typically very difficult to replace, as they have many dependencies attached to them.

What do change frequently are the business processes stitching together the value chains and customer interactions with the core business capabilities, along with the company's product offering and business model.

Process orchestration is an important ingredient to balance the different paces of change in the customer interactions and business model vs. the core IT systems of record. It also allows organizations to easily pull in new capabilities, provided as separate tools or SaaS services (see Figure 9).

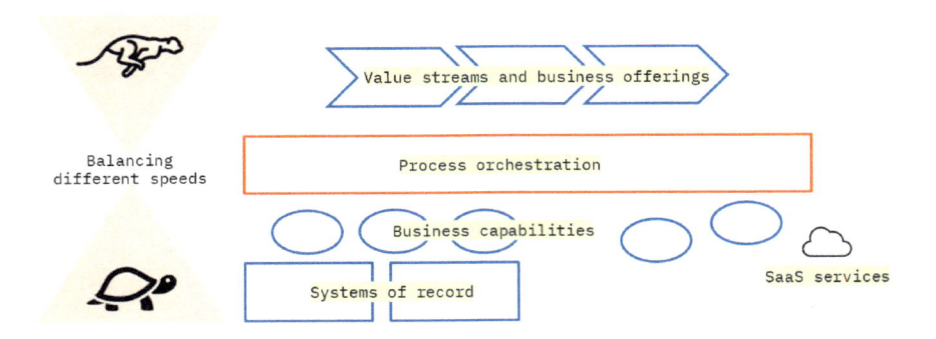

Figure 9: Process orchestration stitches together new and existing business capabilities into end-to-end processes

An example may help to illustrate this. Suppose your car insurance company provides a new app for submitting claims. The app allows you to attach pictures of the damage along with documents like invoices. It guides you through everything you have to do to get your claim settled, giving you immediate feedback when you upload your photos and providing an estimate of the payout you will receive. In the happy case, you get paid within minutes or hours.

This functionality is not part of the core insurance systems. Instead, the app on the frontend is very likely a custom-developed component that uses some core business capabilities (e.g., to retrieve customer and contract data, create claims, trigger payouts, etc.). At the same time, the claim settlement process requires orchestration of not only these tasks, but others as well (e.g., determining responsibility, estimating damages, making payments). The orchestration layer allows you to add new tasks or adjust the process easily, even allowing you to experiment, for example, with new AI capabilities. Still, all the important data and the core business functionality is provided by the existing core systems.

Process orchestration thus allows organizations to innovate business models and improve their processes, without having to replace all of their legacy infrastructure at once. This in turn allows customers to benefit from new service offerings, better transparency, and faster cycle times, all of which greatly improve the customer experience.

Operational Efficiency

In addition to being innovative, staying cost-efficient is also a priority for many organizations, especially when they need to grow their business while keeping operating expenses under control. And while customers are always looking for a better experience across multiple channels, businesses can't always charge their customers for this. In fact, often they cannot. This creates further pressure on operating margins and forces organizations to drive efficiency in operations.

Process automation in general drives operational efficiency by, for example:

- Decreasing the amount of human involvement thanks to straight-through processing
- Reducing the time spent manually routing requests
- Reducing the amount of rework and reassignment (rerouting)
- Reducing manual and duplicate data entry into systems

In addition, **process orchestration** in particular provides insights into what is going on, allowing both technical and business operation teams to:

- Identify areas of high human involvement as candidates for automation.
- Allocate available resources where the highest volume of business is observed.
- Identify technical incidents quickly and derive and apply appropriate fixes quickly, removing stuck processes and clearing up customer inquiries.
- Identify gaps in business projections and real-life execution in order to adjust in an agile way.

Process orchestration technology gives you all of that right out of the box—a huge advantage when, as is so often the case, you simply don't have the time and resources to gain these insights through process mining or big data analytics solutions. Process orchestration opens the door for continuous delivery and improvement of processes.

Faster Time to Value and Greater Business Agility

Business requirements change continuously and rapidly, requiring companies to adjust fast and modernize their infrastructure to stay competitive. A rigid or chaotic implementation of processes and rules (hardcoded, or with complex choreography) can become a serious impediment for business agility and project cycle times. Technology leaders like CIOs therefore need to reduce the cycle time for automation projects and make sure they provide value to the organization as quickly as possible.

The agility that good process orchestration technology brings to the table is achieved through two things:

- A common language for processes
- Developer-friendly tooling

Let's look at these one by one. The first key element is a standardized graphical model to express business processes. In an earlier example we used BPMN, an internationally adopted ISO standard from the Object Management Group (OMG) for process models that are not just modeled graphically, but can also be executed by an orchestration engine.

This is a real superpower: with BPMN you can draw graphical process diagrams that can be understood by various stakeholders in your organization, and those diagrams are not dead documentation artifacts, but actually the source code of running software systems. This means that you can see any runtime incidents, or also statistical data, visualized on top of those process diagrams. If you want to change a process, you know exactly how it is implemented today and have a great tool to demonstrate and discuss possible modifications.

BPMN is also a very powerful language. It implements many advanced workflow patterns[14], which means that you can directly express situations that occur with real-life processes elegantly in BPMN without the need for clumsy workarounds that make process models hard to understand. (You can find some examples in "Why process orchestration needs advanced workflow patterns,"[15] on the Camunda blog.)

In short, BPMN is a great choice for process modeling; we are not aware of any other language that provides this triad of easy understandability, broad industry adoption, and powerful execution semantics.

We concentrate on process orchestration in this book, but if process orchestration is Batman, it must have a Robin. Process orchestration's sidekick is *decision automation*. Decision automation requires creating business-readable decision models, typically expressed as decision tables in the OMG Decision Model and Notation (DMN) standard. As you might expect, the ideas behind DMN are pretty close to BPMN; what's more, BPMN process models can natively invoke DMN decisions, and some tools support both standards.

The advantage of a common language and understanding should not be underestimated. One project manager in a customer's context once told us that while they now put in 20% more effort in the early analysis phases, as the graphical process models trigger more discussions, they save roughly 10 times that effort in the implementation, because the requirements are pretty clear by then. This is in line with the findings of a well-known study by the Systems Sciences Institute at IBM[16]: problems found during tests are **15 times more expensive** to fix than problems found during design.

Another good perspective to view this from has to do with the lifespan of software. Automated core processes will be in operation for at least a couple of years (different studies commonly report numbers between 4 and 12 years). Within that time frame, you will need to make adjustments to the processes, quite possibly at a point where your people have already forgotten how the software was developed in the first place. A graphical diagram helps everybody involved get up to speed quickly and find the right places to make changes.

Let's briefly get a bit more technical and consider developer friendliness and open architecture. This is one of the main differentiators of the Camunda platform, for example, and it has proven to be incredibly powerful. A developer-friendly platform allows you to apply state-of-the-art software development paradigms while building on existing skills (e.g., Java or C#) and tools (like CI/CD and testing frameworks) instead of spending time learning proprietary languages, and an open architecture lets you easily integrate new and existing technologies (like your ERP or CRM system). A platform with both of these qualities makes it easy for an organization to keep its existing engineering practices in place and simply add process orchestration into the mix, greatly improving time to value. This is in sharp contrast to the technology available a decade ago, namely business process management suites (BPMSs), which were effectively aliens in the IT landscape, leading to very proprietary approaches that hardly anyone understood and typically making everybody quite unproductive.

To give you a concrete example of what faster time to value can mean, T-Mobile Austria has said that it can bring new products to market four times faster[17] thanks to the adoption of a modern process orchestration platform.

Enabling Artificial Intelligence

These days, there's a lot of hype around AI, machine learning (ML), and large language models (LLMs)—but organizations need to be smart about where they can apply these innovations to have an impact on their business. For sure, there will be some experimentation involved.

Process orchestration is a great enabler here, as it makes introducing new software endpoints easy—and AI solutions are always software endpoints. Having an orchestrated process allows you to pinpoint where such services can be introduced, and makes it easy to implement those changes. Without process orchestration, the reality is that processes are kind of chaotic, either manually driven or spaghetti-integrated, which makes it hard for organizations to find the right places to introduce new functionalities (let alone run A/B tests to experiment with new technologies).

So, the process orchestrator is a catalyst for strategically adopting and integrating new technologies like AI. We gave an example earlier around automatically assessing accident pictures and estimating damages in claims processes for insurances, but you can probably think of many more (say, fraud detection in KYC processes).

Without understanding your process and knowing where to integrate AI endpoints, you can't leverage AI properly, let alone use it to transform your business. Process orchestration is table stakes in the AI economy.

Technical Problems Process Orchestration Engines Solve

In addition to the previous benefits, an orchestration engine also simply solves some technical problems that would be hard to solve otherwise and would slow down your IT teams. This is largely about long-running processes, as they require certain technical capabilities. Chief among these are:

- **Durable state (persistence):** The orchestration engine keeps track of all running process instances, including their current state and historical audit data. While this sounds easy, durable state is still a challenge to handle, especially at scale. It also immediately triggers subsequent requirements around understanding the current state, which means you will need operations tooling. An orchestration engine needs to manage transactions, too; for example, handling concurrent access to the same process instance.

- **Scheduling:** An orchestration engine needs to keep track of timing and possibly escalate if a process gets stuck for too long. Therefore, there must be a scheduling mechanism that allows the engine to become active whenever something needs to be done. This also allows tasks to be retried in the event of temporary errors.

- **Versioning:** Having long-running processes means that there is no point in time when there is no process instance running. In this context, "running" might actually mean waiting. Whenever you want to make a change to a process, such as adding another task, you need to think about all the currently running instances. Orchestration engines support multiple versions of a process definition in parallel. Good tools allow migrating instances to a new version of the process definition, in an automatable and testable manner.

Ignoring those requirements and working without an orchestration engine just means that you need to code a lot of those features in your own project, which leads to a lot of accidental complexity and your developers working on issues that do not deliver direct business value. With an orchestration engine, you get all of this for free (Figure 10).

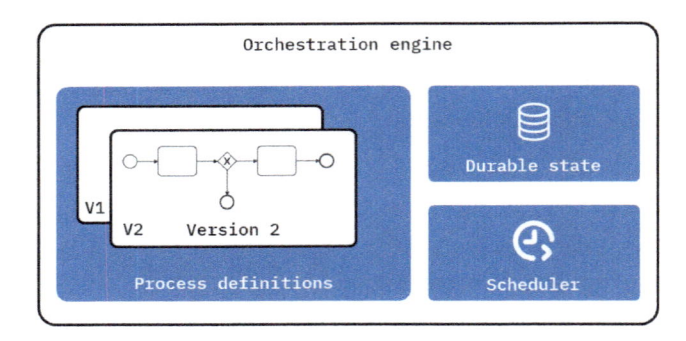

Figure 10: An orchestration engine provides versioning, scheduling, and durable state out of the box.

Understanding Process Types That Can Be Orchestrated

The term *business process* is quite loaded, and of course there is a huge diversity of processes. In this section, we'll attempt to bring a bit of order to that chaos.

Tailor-Made Digital Processes

Let's first sketch out the boundaries of what this book covers. When we talk about process automation in this book, we mean the following processes:

- **Business/digital processes:** These are the typical business processes that are common to most companies (like customer onboarding and order fulfillment), spanning multiple systems end to end. Some people prefer to refer to these as "digital processes," considering the term "business process" somewhat old school.
- **Integration processes:** These are processes that focus on the point-to-point integration of systems or services, for example to orchestrate microservices. There is not a clear boundary between business processes and integration processes, as almost any automated business process will also integrate endpoints. Therefore, we will not differentiate those two categories in this book.

Other types of processes are explicitly out of scope. These include:

- Processes between untrusted participants (such as separate companies). This is a potential setting for blockchain.
- Infrastructure provisioning or IT automation processes (e.g., Ansible, Terraform). This is a domain on its own with specialized tools.
- Continuous integration/continuous delivery processes (e.g., Jenkins, GitHub Workflows). CI/CD build pipelines are standard processes in software engineering that are automated by standard software.
- Internet of Things (IoT) processes (e.g., Node Red). IoT use cases are often tackled with dedicated tooling that we would categorize as task automation software.

It's also important to recognize that there are two very different types of digital or integration processes:

- **Standard processes:** Whenever your company doesn't want to differentiate via the process, you can buy commercial off-the-shelf (COTS) software, like ERP, CRM, or human resources (HR) systems. In this case, you typically adapt your working procedures to the software.
- **Tailor-made processes:** Some processes are unique to an organization and because of that need to be tailor-made to the organization's needs. While these processes might be the same across different organizations (e.g., customer onboarding, order management, claim settlement), the way the organization designs and implements them is unique and can help differentiate them in their market. This enables organizations to be more competitive, conduct their business more efficiently, reduce costs, increase revenue, and transform into a more digital business. Sometimes, the uniqueness also simply stems from a zoo of bespoke legacy systems that need to be integrated!

There is some overlap between these two categories when you customize your standard software, but companies have become more and more cautious about doing this because of bad experiences in the past.

The decision on the type of the process needs to be made separately for every process in the company. There's no right or wrong choice, as long as your decision reflects your business strategy.

To recap, Figure 11 shows the types of processes you might encounter, and zooms in on the ones we're focusing on here.

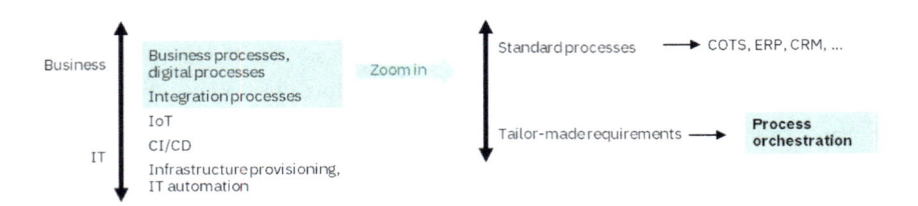

Figure 11: The diversity of processes in an organization, and the ones this book focuses on automating

Diversity of Business Processes

You can use process orchestration for a huge variety of use cases (Figure 12). The use cases with the biggest value are core end-to-end business processes, like customer onboarding, order fulfillment, claim settlement, payment processing, trading, and the like. But customers also automate smaller processes. These processes are less complex, less critical, and typically less valuable, but they're still there, and automating them will have some return on investment (or may simply be necessary to fulfill customer expectations). Good examples are master data changes (e.g., address or bank account data), bank transfer limits, annual mileage reports for insurance, delay compensation, and so on.

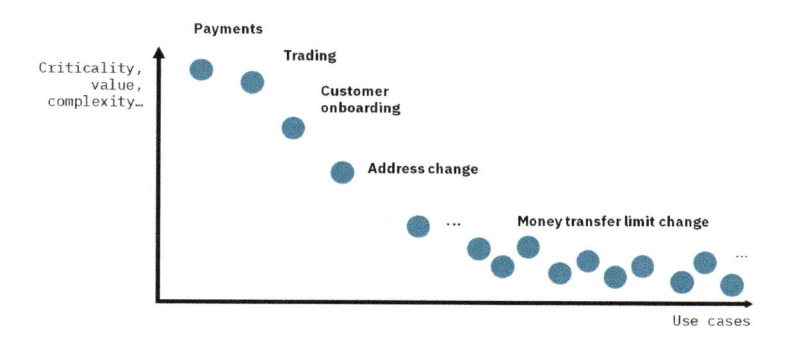

Figure 12: Process != process—there are typically some highly critical core processes to automate, but also a long tail of simpler ones.

It's important to recognize that **non-functional requirements might differ** depending on the complexity of the use case. While critical, highly complex use cases are always implemented with the help of software engineering methods, to make sure the quality meets the expectations for this kind of solution and everything runs smoothly, the use cases on the lower end of the spectrum don't have to comply with the same requirements. For example, if a solution is not available for some time, it might not be the end of the world. If it gets hacked, it might not be headline news. If there are weird bugs, it might just be annoying.

A Useful Categorization of Use Cases

The important thing is to make a conscious choice and not apply the wrong approach for the process at hand. An approach that we have seen work successfully is to categorize use cases and place them into three buckets, which we typically color red, yellow, and green.

Red processes are mission-critical for the organization. They are also complex to automate and probably need to operate at scale. Performance and information security can be very relevant, and regulatory requirements might need to be fulfilled. Often we talk about core end-to-end business processes here, but sometimes other processes might be similarly critical. For these use cases you need to do professional software engineering using industry best practices like version control, automated testing, continuous integration, and continuous delivery. The organization will want to apply some governance, for example around which tools can be used and what best practices need to be applied.

Yellow processes are less critical, but the organization's operations will still be seriously affected if there are problems with these. So, you need to apply a healthy level of governance, but you also need to accept that solutions here may not be created to the same standard of quality as for red use cases, mostly because you simply have a shortage of software developers.

Green processes are often local to one business unit or even an individual. The automations are often quick fixes stitched together to make one's life a bit easier, but the overall organization likely wouldn't realize it if they broke apart. The organization can afford to leave people a lot of freedom when it comes to these noncritical use cases, so typically there is no governance or quality assurance applied.

Figure 13 provides a summary of the different categories.

Category	Description	Non-functional requirements	Value contribution	Governance
Red	Processes that are mission-critical for the organization (typically core end-to-end business processes, but sometimes other processes might be similarly critical)	- Complex to automate - Need to operate at scale - Performance and information security - Regulatory requirements	Very high; large influence on operational efficiency, customer experience, and business agility	Strong governance and quality controls need to be in place (e.g., standardized tooling, development stacks, version control, automated testing)
Yellow	Less critical processes, but ones where the organization's operations will still be seriously affected if there are problems	Depends	Not very high for individual cases, but together the long-tail processes deliver significant value	Require a healthy level of governance
Green	Simple processes, often local to one business unit or even an individual	Low	Very low, on an individual case basis	No governance required

Figure 13: A possible taxonomy of process categories within an organization

Going back to our diverse set of processes, we can now map those to their respective categories, as visualized in Figure 14.

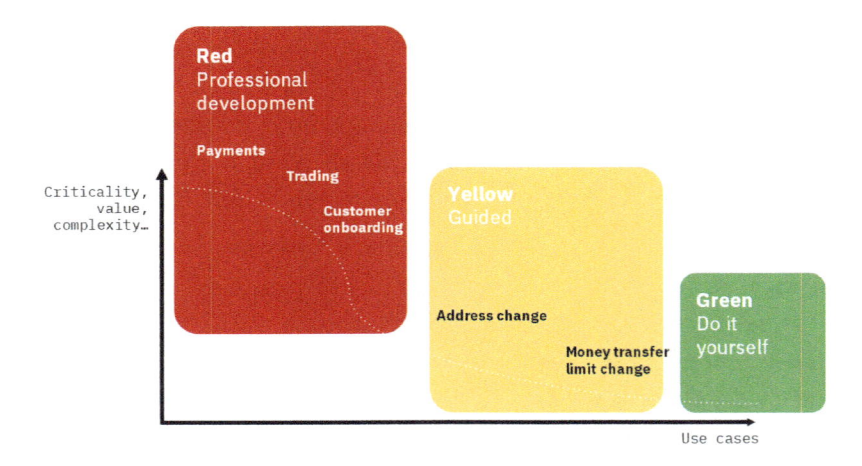

Figure 14: Categorizing processes by their criticality and complexity

Tailoring Your Process Automation Approach

As mentioned previously, when dealing with red use cases organizations typically apply traditional software engineering methods, strict governance, and industry best practices, incorporating a process automation platform like Camunda into those efforts. Green use cases, on the other hand, are usually handled with Office-like tooling or low-code solutions like Airtable or Zapier. The yellow bucket is where the rubber hits the road: this is the long tail of processes that all need to be automated. This requires balancing non-functional requirements and effort, and establishing a fair level of governance, quality assurance, and information security. These processes can be automated with Camunda by making use of low-code accelerators like Connectors[18], rich forms, data handling, integrated tools like Tasklist[19], and browser-based tooling.

A good example of an organization using Camunda to automate both red and yellow use cases is Goldman Sachs. In addition to using the platform as a foundation for automating core banking use cases[20], they have built an extensive low-code platform[21] based on Camunda for the yellow use cases. As those case studies show, they've tackled the solutions quite differently (as a side note, Goldman Sachs built the low-code platform themselves because they started on it several years ago, when there were no out-of-the-box solution accelerators available from Camunda).

In short, solution design, governance, and team structure are different for red and yellow use cases. We'll point this out throughout the book, so we'll refer back to these two categories of use cases often.

Avoiding the Danger Zone Around Vendor Rationalization and Tool Harmonization

Reducing the number of vendors and tools in use across an organization is a common goal. This is understandable on many levels, but it can be very risky if the different non-functional requirements of green, yellow, and red processes are ignored. For example, procurement departments might not want to have multiple process automation tools in use, but they might not fully understand the difference between a platform like Camunda and a low-code platform. And while teams may be able to argue why they can't use a low-code tool for red use cases (as those tools simply don't fit into professional software development approaches), it gets more complicated for yellow use cases.

This can lead to a situation where low-code tools that are made for green use cases are applied to yellow ones. Whereas this might work for simple yellow processes, as Figure 15 shows, it can become risky if the processes are more complex, or simply if organizational requirements around stability, resilience, ease of maintenance, scalability, or information security rise over time. On the other hand, Camunda's low-code acceleration features seamlessly extend its sphere of usability into yellow use cases: you don't have to involve software developers for everything, but you know that if additional non-functional requirements arise you'll be able to fulfill them, as the platform is built for red use cases. For example, if a solution starts to get shaky you can easily add automated tests, and you can easily scale operations if you face an unexpected spike in demand (think of flight cancellations around the time of the Covid-19 pandemic; this was a yellow use case for airlines, but practically overnight it became highly important to be able to process them efficiently).

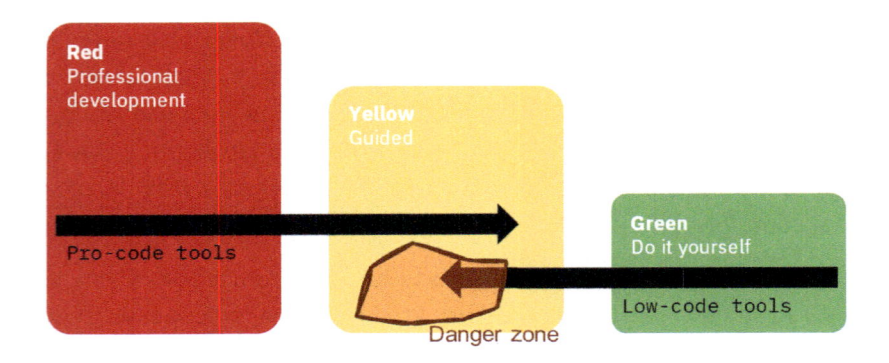

Figure 15: Using low-code tools to automate yellow use cases can be risky, especially if non-functional requirements change over time

To summarize, it's far safer to target yellow use cases with a pro-code solution like Camunda, which has added low-code acceleration layers that you can (but don't have) to use. This allows you to use a single process orchestration stack for a large variety of processes, while avoiding getting stuck with low-code solutions that cannot cope with changing non-functional requirements.

Typical Use Cases for Process Orchestration by Industry

TODO: Refine section

Financial Services

Let's look at some typical process orchestration use cases in the financial industry.

Streamlining the mortgage application process

Financial institutions orchestrate multiple processes to ensure a smooth customer experience. Picture a customer applying for a mortgage online. Through process orchestration, the journey from initial application through document verification, credit checks, underwriting, and finally loan approval is made seamless. The outcome is a happy customer who values an expedited, effortless process.

Goal: Seamless customer journeys

Technical process metric: Application processing time, error rate in applications

Business process metric: Customer satisfaction (CSAT) score, net promoter score (NPS), conversion rate

Automating claims processing

Organizations in the financial services sector handle various interconnected processes, like initiating loans, setting up new accounts, and processing claims. Orchestrating these processes streamlines workflows, automates routine tasks, cuts out unnecessary steps, and minimizes mistakes. As a result, staff members are freed to concentrate on more significant tasks, boosting productivity and leading to cost reductions.

Goal: Enhanced operational efficiency

Technical process metric: Average handling time (AHT), rate of manual interventions

Business process metric: Cost per claim, claims processed per full-time equivalent (FTE), CSAT, NPS

Know your customer (KYC) or anti-money laundering (AML) compliance checks

In the highly regulated financial services sector, adhering to compliance standards is essential. Process orchestration aids in consistently meeting regulatory demands by automating compliance verifications, managing documents, and keeping audit records. This approach lowers the risk of noncompliance, possible penalties, and damage to reputation, building trust among both customers and regulatory authorities.

Goal: Improved compliance and risk management

Technical process metric: Compliance error rate, average time to complete compliance checks

Business process metric: Number of compliance incidents, regulatory fines incurred

Launching a new product, e.g. an investment offering

In a competitive environment, the quick introduction of new products and services is crucial. Process orchestration speeds up time to market by simplifying the processes of product development, pricing, and approvals. For example, coordinating the launch of an investment product requires synchronizing tasks across various departments, including product management, legal, marketing, and compliance. This leads to faster innovation, the capability to quickly capitalize on market opportunities, and increased competitive differentiation.

Goal: Faster time to market

Technical process metric: Time from concept to launch, number of iterations before launch, cycle times

Business process metric: Faster launch times, market share percentage and velocity

Supporting a surge in transaction volumes

Financial institutions are required to adjust to shifting market trends, evolving client needs, and new technologies. Process orchestration offers the adaptability to alter processes accordingly, so the organization can respond quickly to market changes. As companies develop and broaden their operations, process orchestration scales smoothly, accommodating higher transaction volumes and growing service offerings.

Goal: Agility and scalability

Technical process metric: Transaction processing time, system uptime/downtime

Business process metric: Improved customer satisfaction, customer retention rate

Todo: Next Industries...

Part 1: Vision

Now that we've explored process orchestration, the value it can bring, and typical use cases, let's turn our attention to using that knowledge to build a compelling vision for your process orchestration initiative.

We'll kick things off with a not-so-nice story, as often you can learn more from failures than from successes. A while ago, we agreed on a strategic collaboration with a large infrastructure provider in Europe. They'd already had some initial success stories with Camunda, and the CIO wanted to set up a centralized process orchestration platform to increase process automation rates, harmonize tool stacks, and accelerate time to value for future initiatives. Efficiency was only one concern; the ultimate goal was to advance hyperautomation across the organization to ensure business continuity with the looming threat of demographic change in the decade to come.

We had a few meetings with the CIO to better understand the company's challenges around their strategic vision. We presented how a process orchestration strategy plays into that and how they could advance their initiative through Camunda's technology and services. Ultimately, we aligned on a shared vision, shook hands, and patted ourselves on the back for having done a great job.

Next up, we spoke with the affected business domains with the goal of identifying potential use cases and kicking off concrete projects. But frustrations quickly arose. The first domain had already settled on a specific standard software, because they wanted to act independently from IT. Two other domains didn't consider process orchestration a strategic priority. Only the fourth domain committed to starting with a specific use case, but not with the urgency we had hoped for. All that made us lose the momentum we had built up initially. Consequently, our IT contacts became elusive; they deprioritized the topic because of limited bandwidth, and the initiative began to stall.

There is one core learning from this story: even commitment from the CIO is not enough to ensure successful adoption of process orchestration. It requires buy-in from IT *and* the business. In this example, the roadmap and vision had been crafted within IT, without involving senior leadership from the business domains. This led to a lack of understanding of the potential of process orchestration and a lack of commitment, which resulted in a lack of urgency in the respective domains.

This chapter will guide you through how you can avoid these and other pitfalls and set up a successful process orchestration initiative that can truly transform your organization.

Luckily enough, in this particular case things still turned out well, as we still had a CIO that believed in process orchestration. We sat down with senior IT leaders, adjusted our approach, and initiated a close dialogue with senior business leaders to course-correct the collaboration and reignite the bold vision that had been set, getting us back on track.

Strategic Alignment: Bridging Vision, Strategy, and Stakeholders

As the story we just recounted illustrates, to set up your process orchestration journey for success you need to:

- Clearly define the scope of your initiative.
- Understand which use cases can benefit from process orchestration across the different domains.
- Link any projects to your corporate strategy.
- Align the expectations of different stakeholders across the organization.
- Repeatedly convey the value and potential of process orchestration across the enterprise, not only to IT stakeholders, but also to the business domains.
- Create a mutual vision and roadmap, involving IT *and* business leadership, that is aligned on how process orchestration will transform your organization.

Let's dive into this in more detail.

Scoping Your Transformation Journey

Sometimes the path is the goal, but when you aim to transform your organization through process orchestration, you'd better have a clear target state in mind. Defining that target state begins with deciding on the scope of your initiative. In other words, which areas of the business do you want to focus your efforts on?

Process orchestration can be applied on different levels, as indicated in Figure 16:

- Enterprise-wide
- Business domains or end-to-end customer journeys (e.g., in banking, commercial vs. business banking)
- Specific business capabilities or processes within a business domain (e.g., a credit origination process)

- Local subprocesses within a business capability or process (e.g., a customer background check within a credit origination process)

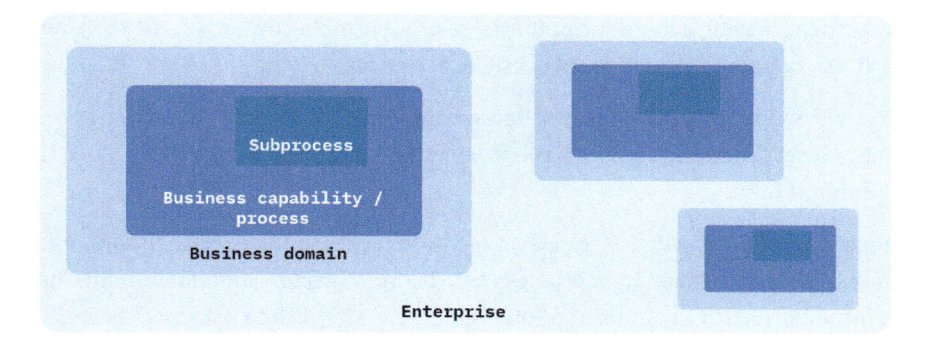

Figure 16: Potential scopes of process orchestration initiatives

We recommend focusing your journey on using process orchestration at the enterprise or business domain level (depending on the size of your domain and the corresponding customer journey). This is because when it comes to automation, it's important to think globally instead of locally. While a quick fix like using RPA to automate one task in a process might work in the short term, such point solutions will prevent organizations from effectively implementing end-to-end processes in the long run. By drawing a global scope, you will also make it easier to achieve the economies of scale needed to build sustainable competitive advantages through process orchestration, without getting bogged down in a myriad of minor initiatives with marginal impact.

This makes the strategic adoption of process orchestration a top management play. For an enterprise scope, the initiative should ideally be sponsored by the C-suite in order to ensure prioritizing investments and executing on the vision. For domain transformations, the initiative should be sponsored by the VPs or SVPs of the respective units. As we mentioned earlier, however, it's crucial that you have both IT and business leaders on board. IT typically makes the technical magic happen, but the business domains will leverage the technology to create business value, which means they need to understand why they want to use it.

Very often, we see process orchestration being tied to existing strategic initiatives (for example, around digitalization, cloud migration, or generally automation). That's normally a good thing, as it can have the advantage of being able to leverage existing funding and momentum.

Defining Your Vision

Once you've defined the scope of the initiative, the first thing you have to do is to develop a clear vision of what you plan to achieve within that scope. While it feels like we're stating the obvious here, it is astonishing how many process orchestration initiatives are not properly grounded in a clearly defined vision. Without such a vision, it will be very hard not only to communicate the why and get buy-in, but also to measure the impact of your initiative. In other words, it will be difficult to "get the business on board." Accordingly, in the absence of a vision, your initiative will be merely tactical, leaving a lot of the potential of process orchestration on the table and putting first wins at risk of being stopped for other tactical reasons.

With a clear vision in mind, you'll be able to tie your initiative to your enterprise goals, identify appropriate success metrics, and track the ROI of your investments. Hence, it's crucial to invest time and thought here.

In their recent book *Rewired*[22], McKinsey executives Eric Lamarre, Kate Smaje, and Rodney Zemmel lay out what it takes to create a good vision: "Strong vision statements have some common ingredients: an aspiration, often anchored around the customer, as well as a time dimension and a quantification of significant value." The vision must be specific and tied to your business strategy, so that it can provide guidance on how your business will be transformed through technology—in our context, process orchestration.

To craft such a vision, close alignment with all relevant stakeholders is needed. As the McKinsey authors point out, through constant dialogue and dedicated workshops, the leadership teams need to build a shared understanding of the potential a technology (such as process orchestration) offers and how to integrate it into the organization. This relates to the business value and potential use cases for the technology, which capabilities are required, and how to develop a roadmap to build them.

To stress it once more: if the key stakeholders are not aligned on and committed to the initiative, it will be hard to drive adoption across your organization and you will get bogged down in the organizational quicksands.

Next up, we'll look at all the different stakeholders that are involved in a process orchestration transformation journey.

Aligning Your Stakeholders

Ultimately, such a complex transformation journey is a team effort across the whole organization. That's why it is crucial to align everyone's expectations. We think of the diversity of stakeholders in two dimensions, along a vertical and a horizontal axis, as shown in Figure 17.

On the vertical dimension, we group the personas according to their strategic and operational focus in the organization, with the C-suite acting as a governing entity across all domains. Strategy-focused stakeholders usually define the vision and provide the budget, while operational stakeholders execute it. In that sense, it's important to link the strategic goals of the organization to the initiative and think about how you can not only enable operational stakeholders to drive adoption across the organization, but also amplify their voices in order to generate a flow of fresh ideas and make sure their valuable experiences are leveraged for further improvements.

Along the horizontal axis, we think in the heuristic of IT and business stakeholders, as well as the multiple domains across the organization. For now, this distinction between "business" and "IT" is helpful to understand the different focus points, mindsets, and motivations. In some digitally mature organizations the distinction between business and IT is eroding, as it should be, in order to deliver business value at scale (we will tackle this topic further in the next chapter). But in reality, for most organizations, business and IT are still operating as different entities that need to be aligned.

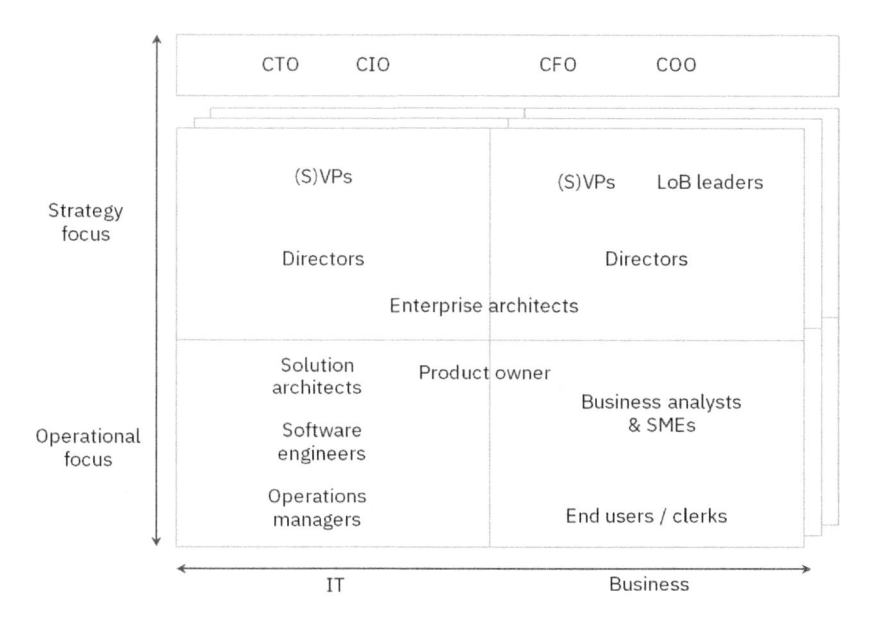

Figure 17: Alignment is required among diverse stakeholders across the enterprise.

If you're targeting an enterprise transformation initiative, it's crucial to have a shared understanding in the C-suite about the potential of the technology and how to tie it to the business strategy. This helps to ensure the necessary funding and leadership to drive this change. Continuing to the (senior) vice presidents, line of business (LoB) leaders, and directors, it is equally important to understand their goals and challenges and to make them aware of the value such a transformation holds. As you will typically start with a few use cases in a few domains (1–3), you'll want to focus on those leaders first so as not to overstretch your capacity. But of course, you should always be open to talking to anyone who approaches you about the value of process orchestration!

Let's look at how a vision for a process orchestration initiative could be crafted in an organization such as a large bank:

C-suite/senior leadership:

- **Objective:** Define the global enterprise vision for process orchestration and automation.

- **Example:** "Our vision is to deploy process orchestration globally to enhance customer experience, enabling faster response times, personalized interactions, and seamless service delivery."

SVP/LoB leader (e.g., of commercial and retail banking):

- **Objective:** Transform the domain/business unit according to the vision.
- **Example:** "Our objective is to leverage process orchestration in commercial and business banking to streamline operations, reduce manual errors, and accelerate transaction processing, ultimately enhancing client satisfaction and loyalty."

Process/product owner (e.g., for the credit origination process in commercial and retail banking):

- **Objective:** Improve processes and products based on strategy.
- **Example:** "The objective is to implement process automation in the credit origination process to minimize approval times, decrease error rates, and improve overall efficiency, ensuring faster access to credit for clients and enhancing their experience."

You should also directly define **metrics** to be tracked. This will most likely happen on the process/product owner level, as you can define very specific metrics that are tied to the business value there. For example:

- **Average approval time:** Measure the average time taken from the initiation of a credit application to its approval, aiming for a significant reduction post-automation implementation.
- **Error rate in credit applications:** Track the percentage of credit applications with errors or discrepancies pre- and post-automation, aiming for a decrease in error rates as automation reduces manual input and enhances accuracy.
- **Customer satisfaction (CSAT) score for credit origination:** Conduct regular surveys or use other feedback mechanisms to gauge customer satisfaction specifically related to the credit origination process, aiming for an improvement in CSAT scores post-automation as a reflection of smoother, faster, and error-free experiences.

Those metrics need to be reported back to the owner of the initiative and the strategic sponsors. For this, you'll require some governance to steer your initiative.

Implementing Change

When applied on an enterprise level, process orchestration can touch hundreds of processes across all domains. Accordingly, you need to manage this change properly. First and foremost, it's important to identify all the relevant stakeholders and understand their motivations. Then you need to communicate a lot and enable as many people as possible to understand process orchestration and its benefits. The more people you can mobilize, the more successful your initiative will be.

Understanding Personas

Let's start with a list of the various personas involved in a typical process automation initiative (Figure 18). The table also indicates the roles that commonly correspond to each persona and their key tasks.

Persona	Typical roles	Tasks
Enterprise sponsor	C-suite, senior leadership For smaller scopes: LoB leaders, SVPs	- Set the vision for the initiative and sponsor it
Initiative sponsor	Business and technology leaders	- Identify business cases in LoBs - Sponsor initiatives in business domains and make sure they get enabled
Strategist	CoE leader, automation initiative owner, IT SVPs, principal architects	- Develop and implement automation strategy - Align stakeholders - Communicate vision
Enabler	Members of a centralized team (CoE), such as IT architects, enterprise architects, solution architects, developers, and business analysts	- Accelerate builders through enablement, reusable building blocks, or internal consulting
Builder	Stakeholders focused on delivering initiatives, preferably in the LoBs or in a centralized team: - IT: Architects, developers - Business: Subject matter experts, business analysts	- Implement solutions - Generate stream of new ideas - Continuous improvement
User	- IT: Operations manager - Business: Clerks	- Ensure day-to-day operations - Provide feedback on potential improvements

Figure 18: Example personas in a process automation initiative

Understanding this role assignment will help you build a communication strategy to empower the right personas to contribute to your process orchestration initiative.

Governing Your Change Process

You need clear accountability about who leads the change, and those leaders need to have a clear idea of how to enable the organization. A typical structure to set this up is a center of excellence (CoE). Whatever you call this (it doesn't have to be called a CoE), it should consist of a dedicated team of experts who drive the strategic, scaled adoption of process orchestration across the enterprise. For now, that definition will suffice; we'll dive more deeply into how to set up a CoE in "Part II: People" starting on page 63.

CoEs are crucial to implementing your enterprise strategy and driving change. They should be led by someone who is capable of articulating the vision broadly across the organization, reporting the value to senior leadership, and helping to identify business use cases. The business, automation, and tech experts in a CoE help enable different parts of the organization to build and implement processes, creating champions across business and IT teams (e.g., within a community of practice, or CoP).

Your initiative might not start with setting up a CoE but instead jump right into concrete business solutions, extracting the learnings into a CoE in a second step. That's totally fine, and often even the better idea, as it will mean you can deliver value faster and use real learnings as the basis for setting up your CoE.

As with most initiatives, ideally you will follow the typical PDCA or Deming cycle[23] for your transformation journey to setup your CoE and implement your vision for process orchestration:

Plan:

- Define vision for process orchestration
- Assess capabilities (which skills and technologies are needed, and which currently exist?)
- Define governance model

Do (communicate):

- Establish communication channels and events to communicate vision
- Build champions across the organization
- Set up center of excellence and community of practice

Do (implement):

- Start executing on your vision
- Build process mindset
- Deliver process orchestration solutions

Check:

- Measure and monitor achieved value of process orchestration solutions
- Communicate value across management levels (vertical) and business domains (horizontally)

Act:

- Improve upon learnings
- Understand challenges and iterate plan accordingly

Figure 19 shows an overview of a typical setup that will help you to drive the needed change in your organization.

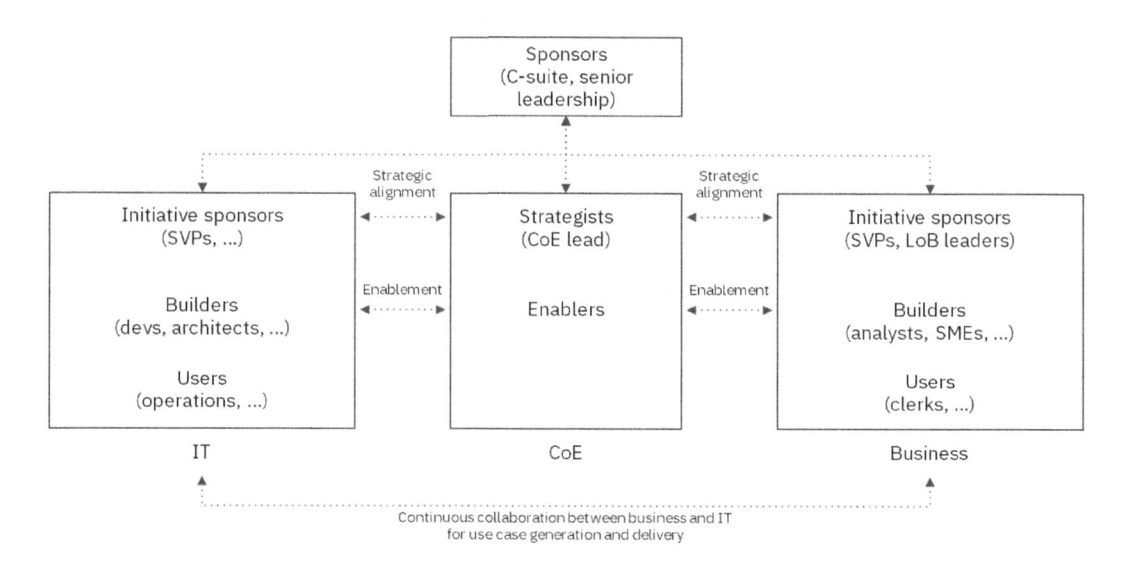

Figure 19: Stakeholders in a typical automation governance setup

In this context, it's also important to understand how decisions about new use cases are made and how they are implemented later on. Strategic initiatives that will transform a business domain and its entire customer journey (e.g., a new end-to-end process in business banking) are typically introduced by *initiative sponsors* (the senior leadership of the respective domains, in this case). They need to align with the *strategist* (e.g., CoE leader) and to some degree the *builders* to define what is possible, as well as the desired outcomes and scope of the initiative. Delivery is then handled by the builders, who within their domains can also often autonomously decide to integrate process orchestration for other use cases (e.g., transforming a specific business capability, such as the credit origination process microservice).

Why Change Fails and How to Avoid This

On the journey to implementing their process orchestration vision, we often see organizations facing challenges or concerns that can easily be addressed by proactive communication and creating the right narratives for change. Let's quickly go over the main challenges.

Fear of automation and job loss

The fear of losing jobs because of automation is a concern as old as automation (or, back in the day, mechanization) itself, as exemplified by the luddites who opposed the advances of the Industrial Revolution. The current strides in AI have reignited this concern. And while efficiency is certainly one key aspect of process orchestration, given the current megatrend of demographic change, it is safe to say that most businesses simply need to automate to ensure business continuity and growth within the scope of their available resources.

As the journalist and blogger Noah Smith (aka Noahpinion) points out in his blog[24], this aligns with macroeconomic research showing that economies and businesses that embrace technological change (read: automation) actually create more wealth and jobs than those that don't. Ultimately, everyone likes to work for a company that prospers, and no employee likes to work with inefficient and broken processes. Embracing process orchestration helps employees focus on higher-value work requiring genuine human skills such as problem solving, creativity, and interpersonal skills (see the Bain & Company article "Automation's Ultimate Goal: The Augmented Workforce"[25]). To disperse the concerns of job loss, communicate this proactively and invite as many people as possible to partake in your transformation initiative.

Speed and cost of solution delivery

Delivering solutions on time, within budget, and with a reasonable ROI is crucial for the acceptance of the initiative within the organization. But failures can happen, and for a multitude of reasons (ranging from poor project management to bad scoping to improper resource allocation). In the context of process orchestration initiatives, we often also see CoEs that are too focused on central delivery, which causes bottlenecks, which in turn can make it inefficient for the different LoBs to automate use cases.

To counter this, aim for federated solution delivery with a state-of-the-art CoE that acts as an enabler and accelerator for those teams (we will discuss this further in the "Part II: People" starting on page 63). If your organizational structure doesn't permit federated delivery, for example because the LoBs don't have IT resources (typically the case in smaller and digitally less mature companies), review your cost accounting structure to make sure there is no incentive in the CoE to inflate costs.

Legacy mindset: IT seen as a service provider/cost center

Cross-functional business and IT teams are the name of the game in state-of-the-art software delivery. But the reality in a lot of organizations is that IT is still seen as a pure service provider. Process orchestration offers a way to overcome this, but it requires a mindset shift. Instead of just drafting requirements and expecting IT to deliver on them, it is necessary for the business to be closely involved in all parts of the initiative: from idea generation to modeling processes to testing early iterations of the implementation to the subsequent operation and continuous improvement of those processes.

This means that when crafting your vision, you need to be sure to give as many people as possible a stake in the initiative through enablement, upskilling, the right tools, and open communication channels through which to submit their ideas. And if you want to reach the highest maturity levels, you need to provide tech-savvy business users the tools and connectors they need to autonomously automate as many processes as possible (we will discuss this approach further later in this book).

Difficulty identifying use cases

Somewhat counterintuitively, despite the constant drive for efficiency and innovation, it's not uncommon for organizations to face the challenge of a lack of new use cases for process orchestration. In this scenario, delivery teams are established but have no new projects on the horizon, leaving them partially idle. Given that the availability of IT resources is typically the bottleneck, the irony is evident, especially considering the challenges companies currently face (from cost pressures and evolving customer expectations to demographic shifts and regulatory demands).

This challenge often points to a fundamental lack of awareness of the value of process orchestration within the organization. Addressing it requires a strategic approach: automation strategists and senior leadership, or what we refer to as initiative sponsors, need to collaborate closely to create compelling business cases. These cases should not only highlight the potential benefits of automation but also outline how it aligns with broader organizational goals and challenges.

For projects of medium complexity, it's essential to open up communication channels between builders (those responsible for implementation) and users (those who will benefit from automation) to capture their improvement ideas. This inclusive approach, focusing on continuous improvement, ensures that the automation pipeline remains aligned with the evolving needs and opportunities within the organization.

Not addressing the chasm

In his book *Crossing the Chasm*[26], Geoffrey Moore talks about a division between different groups of users and customers: on the one hand you have the innovators and early adopters that tend to jump on new product ideas early, but then you have to "cross the chasm" to reach the majority of the market (some of whom will be more willing than others to get on board). In addition, there are likely to be some laggards who will never come around, even if the majority of people embrace it.

This is a powerful mental model that you can also apply internally when bringing concepts like process orchestration into your organization. Specifically, you need to focus on identifying the innovators and early adopters to build your first successes, and only then try to bring on board the majority in the organization. A customer once described this as "riding on the success wave." At the same time, it's important to ignore the potential laggards at the beginning and make sure their negativity doesn't harm your initiative.

The Process-First Mindset

Most of the challenges outlined above can be mitigated by building a *process mindset* throughout your organization, where everybody is aware of the potential of process orchestration. Many organizations do this by providing modeling tools and actively promoting them within the business domains, so that builders can take over modeling larger parts of the value chain of an automation initiative. This leads to closer collaboration between business and IT, makes new use case generation easier, and enables better time to value for those projects.

It's equally important to facilitate the developer experience by providing centralized artifacts and platforms to reduce their cognitive load. Thanks to the varying complexity of processes to be automated, you can also enable tech-savvy business users to develop their own use cases (we will look into the distinction of those use cases shortly).

Finally, a group that is sometimes forgotten but that is very important if you want to continuously improve your processes is clerks and frontline employees. They know how well (or badly) processes are working in practice, so they're a great source of ideas. With the shortage of skilled workers around the world, you want to retain your employees and not have them suffering working with bad processes. Give them the opportunity to fix those processes with you.

In short, the process mindset should extend throughout the entire organization, from the C-suite to the process users themselves (see Figure 19). This will ensure strong leadership buy-in, acceptance of your transformation initiative across all management levels, and a steady flow of ideas for new initiatives, as well as faster time to value through closer business and IT alignment.

TODO: Develop this section further.

Building Your Transformation Roadmap

So, you've created a shared vision for process orchestration with input from all the key stakeholders, and everyone understands how it can transform your enterprise. Great! Now let's see how you can make this vision reality with your transformation roadmap.

Understanding Process Orchestration Work Streams

It's important to differentiate between two separate types of work streams in an organization when adopting process orchestration. We call them the *enterprise work stream* and *delivery work streams*. Organizations typically have one overarching enterprise work stream that enables the delivery work streams. Multiple delivery work streams can exist simultaneously, depending on the level of adoption. A well-crafted enterprise work stream will remove friction for the delivery teams. Figure 20 shows the responsibilities of each type of work stream.

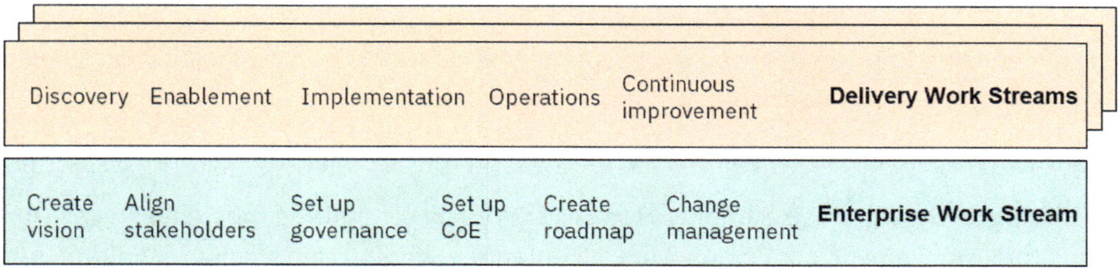

| Discovery | Enablement | Implementation | Operations | Continuous improvement | | **Delivery Work Streams** |

| Create vision | Align stakeholders | Set up governance | Set up CoE | Create roadmap | Change management | **Enterprise Work Stream** |

Figure 20: Process orchestration work streams

The strategic adoption journey starts in the enterprise work stream. This is where you create your vision, align your stakeholders, and align with business leaders to identify processes and customer journeys to be orchestrated. In this work stream you will also evaluate technology, often with the help of an architecture board—for example, deciding on a suitable process orchestration platform—and set up that technology to serve the wider organization. Later in your journey, you will also build governance structures like a CoE in this work stream (see "Part II: People" starting on page 63).

As a quick side note, big international organizations with hundreds of thousands of employees might actually even distribute that one enterprise work stream by having a central, global CoE and some federated local CoEs. This is driven by practical concerns, as one central unit could easily be overwhelmed by too many requests and would not be able to provide a localized experience to internal customers, either time zone–wise or culturally.

Developing and deploying concrete solutions takes place within one or more delivery work streams. These may be driven by the enterprise work stream, especially when you're just getting started and want your CoE to be directly involved in the first use cases. Conversely, sometimes an enterprise work stream is only derived after a first successful lighthouse project, so you might implement one or two delivery work streams before amplifying the vision to the enterprise level. In that case, adoption follows a wave pattern: organizations start by looking at a specific problem, elevate the solution approach to the strategic level, derive a strategic vision from this, and then get operational again to build additional hands-on projects while evolving a strategic enablement function over time.

Ideally, you'll have multiple cross-functional teams working in parallel on their delivery work streams to avoid bottlenecks. This means you can have multiple delivery work streams in progress, which all follow a similar pattern which the CoE can support:

- Discovery (is the technology a fit for my problem?) and goal definition (what do we want to achieve and how do we want to track it?
- Enablement (building up required process modeling and development skills in the team)
- Implementation (implementing the process orchestration solution)

- Operation (running the solution in production)
- Continuous improvement and value reporting (to capture whether the solution is running smoothly and its value contribution to the organization)

We will elaborate on this further in "Part IV: Delivery" starting on page 149.

And this is exactly where the economy of scale kicks in: by centralizing the right activities (infrastructure, enablement, accelerators) in your enterprise work stream through a CoE, you can establish repeatable playbooks for your federated (read: decentralized) delivery work streams, reduce the developers' cognitive load and letting them focus on what matters—delivering business value.

De-Risking Your Start with Process Tracking

When you're first getting your process orchestration initiative underway, *process tracking* can be a helpful way of lowering the risk.

TODO: Describe tracking: Tracking -> Step by step orchestrate -> improve, as talked about in our keynote at CamundaCon NYC 2023

Enterprise Adoption Phases

We can distinguish three phases in the strategic adoption of process orchestration in an organization and the development of its enterprise work stream: *discovery*, *delivery*, and *scaling*.

Discovery

During the discovery phase, enterprises conduct evaluations and strategic planning to assess the viability of process orchestration. This involves executing proofs of concept (PoCs) to identify a suitable tech stack, aligning objectives with organizational goals, and developing a roadmap for the enterprise journey. Establishing governance structures and defining operating models and team structures are essential steps to ensure effective adoption.

The discovery phase typically encompasses these five steps (for steps 1 and 2, see also "Defining Your Target Operating Model" starting on page 100:

1. Assess your current operation approach.
2. Define your target state and scope.
3. Identify solutions and use cases.
4. Build a roadmap and timeline.
5. Execute on it (deliver first solutions, build a platform and the required skills).

Delivery

In the delivery phase, organizations focus on implementing process orchestration solutions. They design the architecture, set up the chosen platform (e.g., Camunda), and initiate the first use cases. The CoE might be more heavily involved in the first projects, to help with successful implementation and to create a learning effect for the centralized team. After the initial groundwork, a few additional domains (typically one to three) will start to adopt process orchestration, laying the groundwork for scaling up orchestration efforts.

Scaling

During the scaling phase, more delivery work streams are added, expanding process orchestration across the organization. This phase enables enterprises to maximize the benefits of orchestration, improving efficiency and agility. Continuous refinement and optimization ensure alignment with evolving business needs, driving ongoing improvement and innovation. Also, the CoE typically evolves to an extent that yellow use cases are increasingly supported by providing smart low-code features, such as connectors.

Across all phases, it is crucial to provide ongoing communication to all the relevant stakeholders and value tracking for the initiatives through setting monitoring corresponding KPIs for specific use cases (e.g. achieved efficiencies) and enterprise level (e.g. number of use cases in production or number of business cases handled). Communication could happen through internal events such as community meetups, blog posts in your organization's intranet, or in direct conversations between CoE and business leaders. Conveying the achieved value is key in building a process mindset and generating a fresh flow of new initiatives, and sharing lessons learned and best practices will help development teams for future initiatives.

Figure 21 shows an example of what your roadmap might look like, across the three enterprise adoption phases. Per a study by Bain & Company[27], you should aim to achieve a positive ROI about 12–18 months after the start of your initiative.

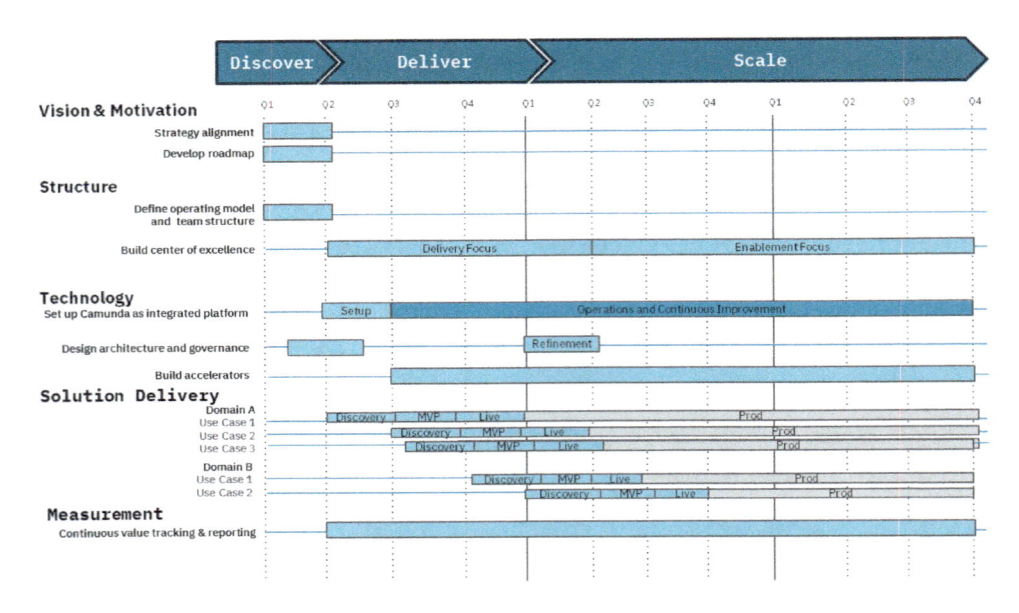

Figure 21: An example enterprise adoption roadmap

Prioritization of Use Cases or Domains

It's important not to overstretch your delivery teams at the beginning of your process orchestration journey, so you'll want to start just with a few selected domains, customer journeys, and use cases.

You'll need to carefully select these first use cases, as they can have a big influence on your overall success. Choose use cases that will help you generate visibility for the initiative, showcase initial value, and build up learnings from which future projects can benefit. We recommend starting with a few high-value use cases of medium complexity that aren't too political. From there, you can gradually work your way up to more challenging use cases.

To help you build up and prioritize your pipeline, we have developed a simple model that you can use to categorize the expected business value and complexity of a given project (which translates to the expected effort). You can apply this model to specific use cases, or use it to assess whole domains. In a nutshell, it will help you place your use cases (or domains) on a simple 2x2 matrix sorted by value and complexity, as shown in Figure 22.

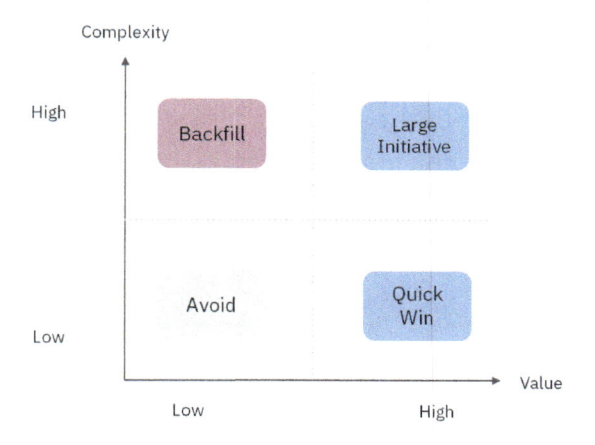

Figure 22: A prioritization matrix for process orchestration projects

On the x-axis, we position use cases (or domains) according to the expected value or business outcome in terms of efficiency, customer experience, or gained business agility. On the y-axis, we look at the complexity. Which use cases (or domains) should you focus on? Of course, the ones on the right, which is where you can reap high-value gains, and especially those in the bottom-right quadrant, where you can get a quick win.

Looking at individual use cases, the complexity is determined by multiple factors. For example:

- How many tasks that require orchestration, and how complex are they?
- How much integration is needed (e.g., how many endpoints and technologies are involved)?
- Do some of the tasks need to be performed by humans, and if so do you have existing human task management software?
- Has a process orchestration tool been decided upon, and is it available to the team?

Looking at the domain level, the complexity is influenced by factors such as:

- The delivery capacity (What is the bandwidth and skill level of the builders in the domain?)
- The maturity of the IT landscape (Do the most important systems have API access? How consistent is the domain data?)
- Executive sponsorship (Is the leadership of the domain aware of the potential of process orchestration and willing to sponsor the initiative?)

TODO: Work on a more in-depth version of the prioritization model incl. spreadsheet calculators.

Sometimes senior management is already aligned on which domains or use cases to begin with. If so, great. If not, however, we recommend choosing the first use cases very carefully in order to build traction. Those use cases will also serve as a foundation to harvest real-world experience, which can be further leveraged to fine-tune the prioritization model and plan your transformation journey.

Once you've kicked things off, taking a strategic, enterprise-wide view of your transformation journey will assist you in monitoring progress. It can be helpful to sketch out a map like the one in Figure 23 that shows your use cases, along with their status and business value..

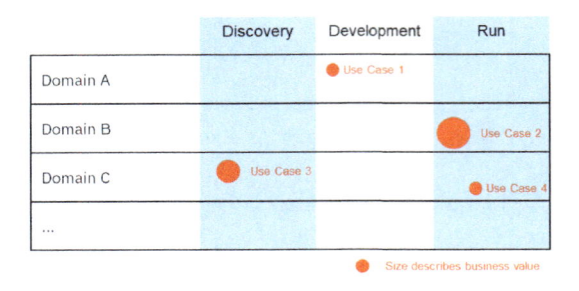

Figure 23: Mapping out your use cases helps you get an overview of your transformation journey.

Amplifying Organic Bottom-up Initiatives

So far, we've discussed a strategic adoption pattern, where the goal is to transform the business from the top down through an enterprise-wide strategy. This is the best approach for unlocking economies of scale as well as competitive advantages on a global (not merely tactical) level.

However, we often see organizations starting their process orchestration journey in a bottom-up fashion. This happens when a specific team or business unit decides to adopt process orchestration technology for a specific use case. Often this decision is driven by IT stakeholders—especially in Camunda's case, where thanks to its open architecture even individual developers might pull to leverage its capabilities, purchasing and operating the platform independently for their current problem at hand. The business case with these grassroots initiatives is typically about saving development effort, as the requirements the process orchestration engine solves would have to be implemented manually otherwise. Sometimes, the engine is also brought in to solve a severe pain point in the current architecture (lack of visibility in event-driven architectures, inability to orchestrate and integrate heterogeneous endpoints in microservices architectures, and the like).

Another flavor of this adoption pattern is when projects already use homegrown state machines, legacy workflow engines, shaky batch solutions, or other orchestration technology that's no longer cutting it, so the developers need to migrate to a more modern or more reliable solution. In this case, the project simply replaces one technology with another to reduce technical debt.

Such a bottom-up journey can be a low-threshold way to get started. Indeed, in our experience, it's not uncommon for there to be multiple independent bottom-up initiatives operating in parallel in bigger organizations. This presents both challenges and opportunities.

On the one hand, there's the challenge of disparate approaches operating in isolation, with no communication between the implementers. Most often, these initiatives also struggle to tie their efforts to the business strategy and measure and communicate the achieved value, even though they may have a positive business impact. Because they do not properly articulate the business value, they can lack the strategic focus and management endorsement necessary for genuine business transformation (although we have observed instances where bottom-up initiatives evolve into top-down initiatives upon reaching critical mass adoption).

On the other hand, there is a great opportunity to build momentum for strategic adoption based on existing success stories. As you don't need to start from zero, you might be faster at defining best practices for implementing new projects. You might also be able to recruit team members to build a CoE that already has firsthand experience with the technology—and you will be able to use existing projects to advertise your initiatives.

One important aspect to understand is that even if you have achieved great results with such individual grassroot initiatives, your process orchestration efforts are flying under the radar of senior leadership. While this is sometimes a good thing, enabling you to move quickly in the early maturity stages of your organization, it bears serious risks. First and foremost, your technology decisions might be called into question, which might impact your ability to mobilize resources around the chosen process orchestration stack.

We encountered a tragic example of this at a company that had successfully automated a lot of its long-tail processes. They'd wired the functionality into their customer portal, so that every customer could trigger an address change process on a self-service basis, 24/7, getting a confirmation just a couple of seconds later. But when the company built a new customer portal, because nobody on the business end had process orchestration top of mind, they didn't even express a requirement for customers to be able to kick off this process. With the release of the new portal, instead of getting instant service, customers who wanted to change their address saw a static web page saying "please call your agent."

This unfortunate case illustrates the need for building awareness around process orchestration throughout the whole organization. By doing so, you ensure that you can secure the resources necessary for a comprehensive transformation. Having multiple bottom-up initiatives in place presents a strong opportunity to get buy-in for an enterprise-wide strategy focused on process orchestration. This often starts with setting up a CoE to harmonize and distribute knowledge, or, in a lower-threshold way, through a community of practice driven by committed individuals without a specific management mandate.

Finding the Golden Path Between Top-down and Bottom-up Adoption Journeys

Both bottom-up journeys and top-down journeys face challenges. The biggest risk with top-down initiatives is that they can be too detached from reality and disconnected from concrete daily challenges. And when you build central teams (like a center of excellence) that are too detached from project work, you can easily end up with ivory towers.

In contrast, bottom-up journeys often fly too far under the radar of senior leaders of the organization, so their strategic potential is not recognized. This in turn can lead to a strategic direction or enterprise architecture in the organization that is not supportive of process orchestration (e.g., instead favoring proprietary and monolithic setups). Also, running multiple bottom-up projects in isolation can result in a proliferation of architecture and tech stacks, which can increase technical debt for the organization.

So, issues can arise with both types of journeys. But in reality, those aren't the only two options. Indeed, we advocate for a hybrid approach: top-down funding and vision, with agile and federated delivery.

Let's explore what this might look like. To start with, you secure a commitment (and funding) from top management to apply process orchestration strategically (top down). After defining a vision with input from a diverse set of stakeholders, you select a small number of actual processes to orchestrate. These projects will address concrete pain points, and they should be tackled in an agile manner—almost like a bottom-up grassroots initiative. The teams working on these early projects will collectively gain experience, defining an architecture, selecting a tool stack, and discovering and documenting good and bad practices. All of these learnings will be harvested so that, after your initial successes, you can quickly build out your CoE—ideally staffed with people involved in those first projects. The CoE will develop a strategy to be applied across the enterprise, which then will help with the delivery of more agile projects.

When visualizing this pattern, we typically use a waveform. It's similar to the approach Gregor Hohpe described for architecting a successful IT transformation: good architects ride the Architect Elevator[28] from the penthouse, where the business strategy is set, to the engine room, where the enabling technologies are implemented.

Questions to Assess Your Maturity

Having equipped you with some tips on successfully building your own vision, we want to close this chapter by considering how you can assess the maturity of that vision and your readiness to get started on your transformation journey. You should be able to answer all of these questions:

- What is the scope of your process orchestration initiative, and what impact do you aim for it to have?

- Have you aligned the crucial stakeholders needed for this initiative? Is the value proposition of process orchestration widely understood among them?
- Do all relevant stakeholders have a shared understanding of where to apply process orchestration?
- Have you set up a governance and change management plan for your initiative?
- Have you developed a roadmap for your adoption journey?
- Have you identified the first solutions to be implemented, which can also serve as pilots?
- Do you have a good overview of concrete solutions that you would like to be created in the next one or two years? Why will process orchestration be beneficial for these use cases? What business outcomes do you aim to achieve?

To help with this evaluation, here is the description of the different maturity levels for vision taken from Figure 3:

- Level 1: Processes are not working efficiently or effectively. Some process tasks may have automated components, but those tasks are too dispersed for the effects of automation to be measured.
- Level 2: Focused on single, mission-critical process orchestration projects, or projects that center around a "broken" process.
- Level 3: Broader, scaled-up initiatives are focused on better business outcomes; measuring success remains a challenge.
- Level 4: Evolving toward a practice where process orchestration supports organization-wide digital transformation goals. This allows harnessing process orchestration to drive strategic business outcomes, at scale and at a rapid pace, for the entire organization.
- Level 5: There's a clearly defined strategy around technology, methodology, and people to execute process orchestration at scale, matched by the ability to execute that vision. A demonstrated track record of delivering strategic value to the organization through process orchestration motivates teams to deliver business transformation at scale.

Part II: People

Process orchestration is largely about automation and technology, but we all know that it starts with people. So, in this chapter we're going to focus on the people that create process orchestration and automation solutions. We'll look at the kinds of people and roles you need, what skills should be developed, and how you can structure your organization to support enterprise process orchestration.

In "Process Orchestration 101" starting on page 19, we described the diversity of use cases for process orchestration and discussed how orchestrating the "red" use cases (complex core processes) requires software engineering. Because of this, we're going to start this chapter with a quick look at how software engineering ideally works today—which is very different from software engineering a decade ago. Unfortunately, these new paradigms are not consistently applied across organizations; like William Gibson famously said in his book *Neuromancer*, "The future is here, but it's not evenly distributed." We hope to encourage more organizations to apply these practices—to distribute this future more evenly—so that they can implement sophisticated process orchestration practices that will allow them to build competitive advantages.

In 2018, Nicole Forsgren, Jez Humble, and Gene Kim published the groundbreaking book *Accelerate*[29], which linked good engineering and DevOps practices to overall organizational measures like profitability, productivity, and market share. In an interview[30] about the book, Nicole Forsgren commented that "the most exciting discovery came during the first year of research, when the team found early evidence that IT performance does matter. This showed that companies with high-performing technology organizations were twice as likely to exceed their profitability, productivity, and market-share goals." (You can find up-to-date numbers in the State of DevOps Report[31] produced every year.)

You don't have to be great at math to know that twice as likely is a huge opportunity—which you also exploit in your process orchestration practice. So let's get going.

How Software Is Being Built Today

Over the last decade, software and the way it is developed have changed dramatically and comprehensively. Let's briefly look at the facets of this change that we consider most important in the context of process orchestration and automation: structure, development methodology, operations, business models, and mindset shifts.

Focused Components That Implement Capabilities

Software systems today are smaller, more modular and focused. Monoliths are rare; instead, we base our systems on focused microservices, a growing number of out-of-the-box SaaS services, and other pieces of reusable functionality. This allows us to concentrate more on the capabilities of a system, rather than looking at monolithic applications. And this in turn allows us not only to adjust the implementation of a capability much more easily and independently, but also to make use of new capabilities and retire outdated ones faster.

Capabilities can be developed and operated as products, and as such they can either be created internally or purchased externally. A product mindset in an organization makes this irrelevant to the consumer of a "capability as a service"; it should be the same experience either way. Getting to this state allows you to choose much more freely what you want to develop in-house—typically things that are really unique to your business or that you want to use to differentiate your offering—and what you simply consume as a SaaS service.

We didn't call this section "Microservices" because, while this is still a hot topic and a good keyword to search for, the microservices architectural style misses the main point we want to make here, which is to provide capabilities as a service. How they're implemented doesn't matter too much. If we'd been looking for a catchier title, we might have gone with "API First," which unfortunately isn't that hip a term any more. It does express the idea of capabilities well, though: you need independent components that provide a technical or business capability via a well-defined API, independent of its concrete implementation (and of whether it is developed in-house or provided externally).

As-a-service thinking allows you to leverage services without knowing how they are operated. This frees the service consumer of a lot of responsibilities, and it works at different levels of abstraction. For example, the typical hyperscalers (Alibaba, AWS, Azure, GCP, etc.) all provide a technical basis for running applications (e.g., containers, application servers, databases) without you knowing about the underlying hardware. And with typical SaaS businesses like those pioneered by Salesforce, you can leverage business capabilities without needing to know how they work under the hood. All of this in turn allows organizations and their development teams to focus on their business problems, and not on running servers and applications. The as-as-service model thus acts as an enabler to create smaller components in a more agile way.

An interesting side effect of this shift is that the business model around software has changed. CIOs no longer buy big, expensive suites with vendor lock-in following sales pitches on golf courses; instead, even powerful C-suite executives need to make sure they have their technologists behind them when making strategic procurement decisions. Software is delivered more and more as a service itself, and subscription models de-risk the use of services for customer organizations. In other words, vendors need to keep providing value if they don't want to be thrown out, and services are combined in a heterogeneous way to build best-of-breed environments.

Agile and DevOps

Agile approaches are the order of the day, even if some organizations or individuals seem to overengineer them a bit (paradoxically rendering them unagile again). The core idea is always useful: creating value through small, iterative steps instead of big bang releases. Agile software development also means including a variety of roles in the development process, breaking down the typical wall between business and IT.

The DevOps movement has also grown enormously over the last decade. DevOps aims to bridge the gap between software development (Dev) and IT operations (Ops). Its primary goals are to increase the speed of software delivery, improve the quality of software releases, and enhance overall operational efficiency. The DevOps movement brought a lot of innovation, from the basics like using version control (it's funny to think that we once had to work hard to convince customers of the importance of this) to automatic build and release cycles, or continuous integration and delivery (CI/CD). Another famous DevOps concept is "you build it, you run it," enabled via technical capabilities as a service, making sure a delivery team really cares about the solution end-to-end (from development to operations).

Process orchestration fits perfectly into this environment. It facilitates agile practices by using graphical models as a basis for discussion, implementation, and operations. It therefore helps to bring the DevOps team more into the business world, making it a true *BizDevOps* team.

Product Thinking

As market pressure and competition increase across all industries, organizations that have been more successful at digital transformation, including automation and software development, are finding themselves far ahead of the pack, resulting in a great deal of pressure on other organizations to catch up.

Catching up requires a fundamental mindset shift in how to approach software development, from a cost center–centric perspective that is largely organized by "IT" as an internal service provider for projects to a more product-led strategy, where business capabilities and value streams are supported by software that is owned by stable teams looking at long-term value creation (rather than focusing on project deadlines and short-term efficiencies). This approach was nicely illustrated in the book *Project to Product*[32] by Mik Kersten.

Thinking about solutions like products means focusing more on the customer journey and the long-term goals, and not so much on the short-term results of a project. Ideally, a team that understands a solution as a product will not only create the first iteration as a project, but also maintain the product over a longer period of time, improving it iteratively. This encourages making sound technical decisions, like choosing boring (but proven) technology[33].

Please note that in this book (and a lot of real-life situations) we still tend to use the term "project," for example when discussing how to create a solution to orchestrate a process. This should not be taken to mean that we prefer the cost-centered approach, but rather that every incremental improvement of a product can be thought of as a project (like a sprint, or an iteration), no matter how small. For example, the "product" might be the customer onboarding value stream. A first iteration might involve setting up the orchestration technology and operating an executable process, but still pushing the tasks to humans. This qualifies as a project, but we find it essential that a product owner and the delivery team keep iterating on the onboarding process and automating the most important tasks next (where "most important" should be defined by business value contribution). Those might be tasks that require a lot of human effort, so automation will make the system cheaper to operate, or tasks where manual completion causes long delays, so automation will improve the customer experience and increase satisfaction. Or it could be tasks that are error-prone when performed manually, so automation can help reduce the risk of regulatory fines. The concrete next step often matters less than the overall approach of thinking in the long term about products. To sum it up: to run successful automation solutions, a product mindset is essential.

Process Ownership

The product mindset also sheds a new light on an old problem in business process management: defining ownership for a business process. The challenge is that most end-to-end processes, or value streams if you prefer that term, stretch across multiple application boundaries as well as departmental boundaries. But organizations are typically structured in functional silos (we don't personally know of any organization that centers its org chart around processes). As a result, there is most often no process owner with real power to improve a process. The result is that nobody looks at processes end-to-end.

Figure 24: Without a clear process owner, nobody has an overview

The worst example one of us experienced was at an insurance company. Asked about the process owner, they came up with a list of more than 20 people that "owned" the customer onboarding process. If there is not one process owner, there is no process ownership.

Product thinking, and an organizational focus on value streams, advocates for solving this problem by assigning clear responsibilities around the business value contributions of value streams to dedicated managers, for example in the form of product owners. We think this is an excellent idea, but we haven't seen it implemented widely or comprehensively yet. Most often, there's an owner on the IT side, but ownership on the business side is lacking. Ideally, organizations should define clear and stable ownership for business capabilities and end-to-end processes that span IT and business (either through two people, or one person having ownership of both). We'd like to challenge you to tackle this opportunity head-on and and hope to present a great success story in the next edition of this book!

Team Topologies

To create successful solutions in your organization, you need to start by looking at who is building and running those solutions. What teams should you have in place? How do they interact? How does that fit into your organizational topology? And how does this align with the abovementioned ideas around agile, DevOps, and product thinking?

We are big fans of the book *Team Topologies*[34] by Matthew Skelton and Manuel Pais, who give great answers to those hard questions. In essence, they make a good case for separating solution building, enablement, and platforms[35]. In that model, productive *stream-aligned teams*, which are autonomous delivery teams maintaining some value stream (equivalent to "product thinking"), require *enabling teams* as well as *platform teams* to make their lives easier. Those supporting teams remove the burden of clarifying all the hard questions around what is called the "undifferentiated heavy lifting": how to set up the infrastructure (including dev and prod environments as well as a CI/CD pipeline), what tech stack to use, how to hook it into the organization's authentication mechanisms, etc. This reduces the cognitive load of the stream-aligned teams, freeing their brains to concentrate on the business problems and leading to business value being delivered much faster.

Looking at process orchestration specifically, we see organizations setting up a dedicated team that not only provides the process orchestration platform, but also the enablement around it—this is the *center of excellence* (CoE) that we will describe later in this chapter. This setup allows the stream-aligned delivery teams to work productively and remain concentrated on delivering business value (Figure 25).

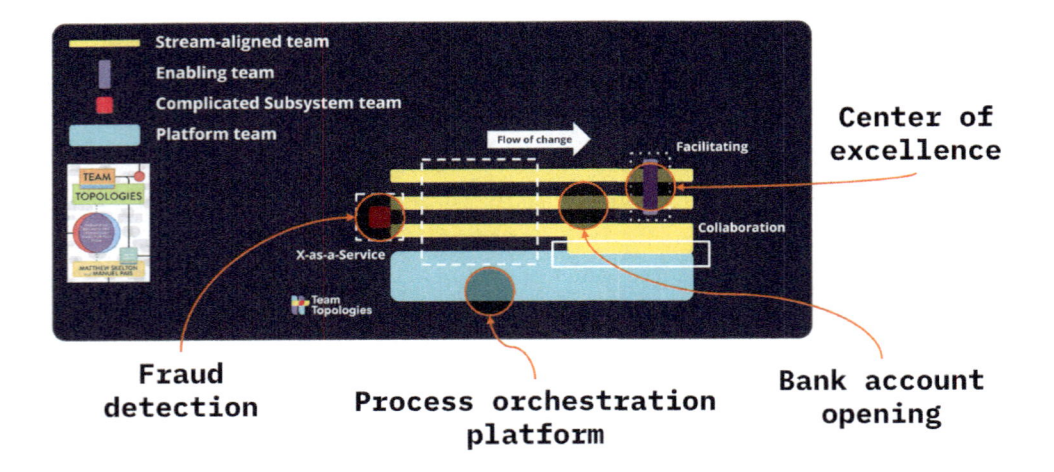

Figure 25: The CoE can take on the role of both platform team and enabling team for process orchestration (as defined in the Team Topologies book).

Diversity of Roles

Going back a decade or two, we had a world where you were either a business person or a developer on the IT side. Business requirements needed to be written down and handed over to a developer to be implemented, and you had teams led by senior engineers doing proper solution design, mixed with juniors that coded and learned. All those roles were rather binary.

This is no longer the case today. The lines between various roles have blurred: a tech-savvy business person can also develop software solutions, especially with the help of low-code tooling or supported by generative AI, and developers are much more diverse in their backgrounds and levels of experience.

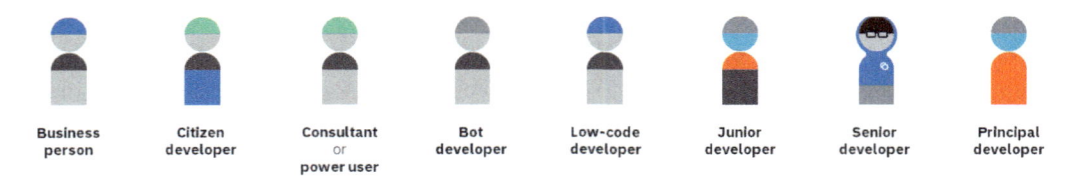

Figure 26: Today, all of these roles can participate in software development

As organizations look to automate more, they need to allow all of those people to take part in software development in some way. We will explore this challenge later in the book, focusing on two key questions:

- How can you enable more non-developers to build solutions? This is basically about adding abstractions and providing a useful low-code layer.

- How can you make sure the (scarce) developers can use their talents in the most effective way? This is partly about providing good team topologies to make them productive, but it is also about allowing them to focus on building components where a developer is needed and relying on other roles to handle the less tech-heavy tasks. For example, senior developers could code pieces of software that are then used in orchestration processes mostly modeled by business analysts. As discussed in "Process Orchestration 101" starting on page 19, this is often much more realistic with yellow processes than it is with processes in the red category, where good engineering practices matter more.

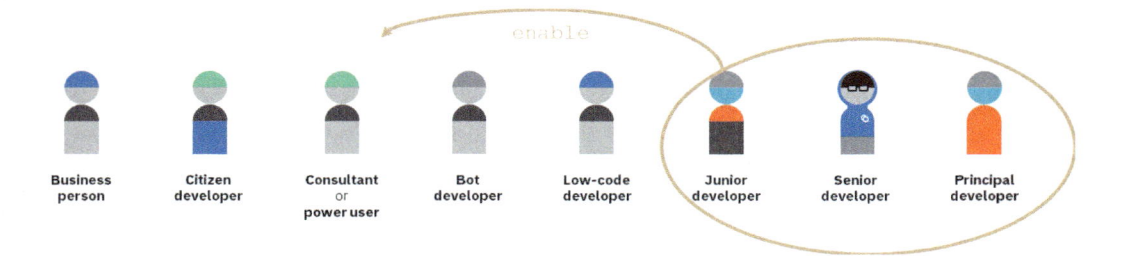

Figure 27: Developers create the components that enable other roles to develop solutions.

A Healthy Level of Centralization

What level of centralization makes sense is a frequent topic of discussion. This may seem to be a hard question to answer, as there are two forces pulling in different directions at the same time: autonomy and independence vs. governance and economy of scale. But this is only a contradiction at first glance—looking at many real-life scenarios, we actually find the answer to be quite clear. Let's start by considering the two questions we always get asked, and our standard replies:

- **Should solutions be created by a central team?** No. Typically we advise against central solution creation, as this becomes a bottleneck quickly. However, there are exceptions to that rule, which we'll address later when talking about the CoE.
- **Should there be a central team to enable and support federated delivery teams?** Yes. We believe that a central CoE that concentrates on enabling is a game changer for success with process orchestration on a broad scale. This central function can do a great deal to reduce the cognitive load of the delivery teams (e.g., running the platform, defining the solution architecture, providing templates, etc.), which will be further described in "The Center of Excellence (CoE)" starting on page 82.

To summarize this rule of thumb: *you should centralize infrastructure and governance but federate delivery*. But this often leads to another question: aren't CoEs too centralized for state-of-the-art software delivery?

There has been a lot of hype around decentralization in software engineering recently, most prominently driven by microservices, domain-driven design, and related methods. This leads to an objection to the CoE concept that goes something like this: "But we just untangled our monolith and moved to independent microservices and value streams so that we could speed up development by having fewer dependencies between teams. Now you're telling us to centralize things again? We don't want to do that; we don't want to have this bottleneck!"

To be honest, it's more than fair to think that because of how CoEs might have been set up in the past. But done right, a CoE blends in seamlessly to state-of-the-art software delivery paradigms, becoming an accelerator instead of a bottleneck. In that sense, the approach is well aligned with all the recent software development paradigms mentioned in this chapter.

Looking at autonomous microservice teams (or whatever the architectural style is in your organization), the core problem without a CoE is that they must figure out many things themselves. The more freedom they have, the more of a burden this becomes. Teams have to evaluate their own tool stacks, define their own solution architectures and approaches, and, in essence, do a lot of technical work that does not implement any business logic. So, the value proposition of the CoE is actually pretty logical: if delivery teams can use an existing platform and have an architecture blueprint for how to design their solutions, they don't have to think about those fundamentals and can dive into delivering business value right away. (Of course, the blueprint needs to provide value for the teams. We'll talk about this later.) This is exactly the platform and enabling function described in *Team Topologies*[36], as mentioned previously.

We see a lot of proof for this point in the market. For example, in the blog post "How We Use Golden Paths to Solve Fragmentation in Our Software Ecosystem,"[37] Gary Nieman from Spotify describes why "rumor-driven development simply wasn't scalable." Spotify gives some more good insights in relation to its Backstage[38] open source project. In essence, too much decentralization started to slow things down because of the resulting complexity. By centralizing services again, they reduced complexity and provided standardization, allowing delivery teams to dive into delivering business logic much faster, without sacrificing their autonomy (see Figure 28). A similar approach is being taken at Twilio[39]: "At Twilio, we do it by offering what we call the paved path. These are mature services that you can just pull off the shelf, adopt, and get up and running super quickly."

The Speed Paradox

At Spotify, we've always believed in the speed and ingenuity that comes from having autonomous development teams. But as we learned firsthand, the faster you grow, the more fragmented and complex your software ecosystem becomes. And then everything slows down again.

The Standards Paradox

By centralizing services and standardizing your tooling, Backstage streamlines your development environment from end to end. Instead of restricting autonomy, standardization frees your engineers from infrastructure complexity. So you can return to building and scaling quickly and safely.

Figure 28: Spotify gives a great summary of why some standardization is necessary to scale.

What you can draw from this is: yes, you should have autonomous delivery teams, and they should work on business logic, often also called domain logic. You should try to find boundaries between business domains that make sense. But you should still provide golden paths (architecture blueprints), central enabling teams, and platforms; otherwise, those teams will drown in technology evaluations and infrastructure tasks. CoEs are crucial to achieving that balance.

Having said this, let's dive into the various possible models of how to deliver solutions in the organization.

Delivery Models

We'll start with the recommendation we just gave: a CoE enabling federated solution delivery. This model is our *greenfield choice*, which means that if there are no good reasons not to, we try to set things up this way. It is a model that typically balances the advantages of centralization with the advantages of federation well. But of course, reality is complex, and there might be very good reasons for you to set things up differently in your organization; so, we will also look at more centralized and more federated options afterward, considering the advantages and disadvantages of each approach.

Federated Solution Delivery with the CoE as an Accelerator

With this approach, you have federated delivery teams and a CoE that does not implement solutions itself, but rather enables the teams within different business units or domains (see Figure 29).

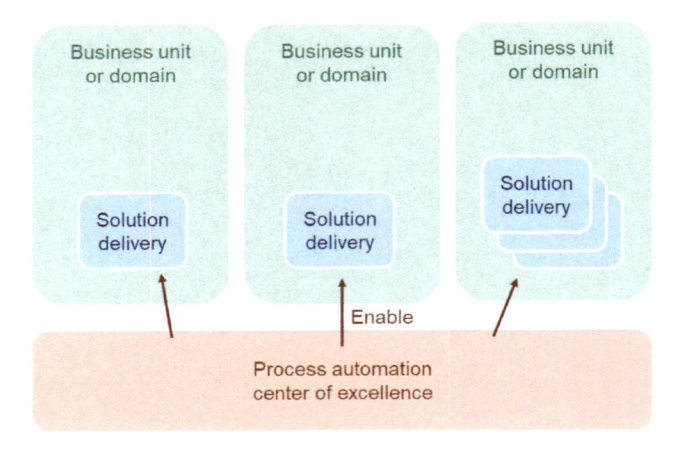

Figure 29: Federated solution delivery with CoE as enabler

Advantages:

- Empowers business-driven automation. Giving ownership to the business domains and their delivery teams enables them to implement initiatives based on their current needs.
- Builds and shares experience and know-how across the whole enterprise.
- Enhances efficiency, as the CoE is building more expertise based on successful projects, helping others avoid pitfalls.
- Enables economies of scale through reusability. Assets and knowledge built up by the CoE can be leveraged across the different initiatives of the organization, allowing for exponential growth (the CoE doesn't become a bottleneck for solution delivery). This also reduces cognitive load.
- Improves governance. As one central team can influence many projects, you can avoid a Wild West setting where every project reinvents the wheel with process orchestration differently. Instead, the best approaches can be reused. Again, this reduces cognitive load.

Disadvantages:

- Centralized authorities might have a bad reputation in your organization (as mentioned in "A Healthy Level of Centralization" starting on page 69), so you might need to overcome that historical impediment.
- The CoE can become a bottleneck when it is too slow to react to internal requests. To avoid this, focus on a strong product mindset and good (internal) customer experience.
- Differences between business units may not be adequately respected (but given that process orchestration technology is horizontal technology, there are typically no big differences in process orchestration in the different organizational units anyway).

- Business domains typically need to have IT expertise in-house (or need to rely on external partners, which might generate problems with knowledge flowing out of the domain again once the partner leaves).

- Sometimes, it is challenging to "make" the domains collaborate with the CoE.

- The CoE must be obsessed with delivering value to the domains. We call this the "pull principle," where working with the CoE makes the lives of the different teams so much easier that they are automatically pulled toward it (as opposed to the "push principle," where teams feel they have to work with a CoE, whether they want to or not). This clearly isn't a disadvantage per se, but it is a challenge.

Fully Decentralized Delivery

Let's contrast the previous approach with a completely decentralized delivery approach without any CoE element. In the worst case, you have silos where domains don't share knowledge with each other. In the best case, you will have a lively community of practice (CoP), where people from different business units meet regularly to exchange experiences (see "What About Communities of Practice (CoPs)?" starting on page 83).

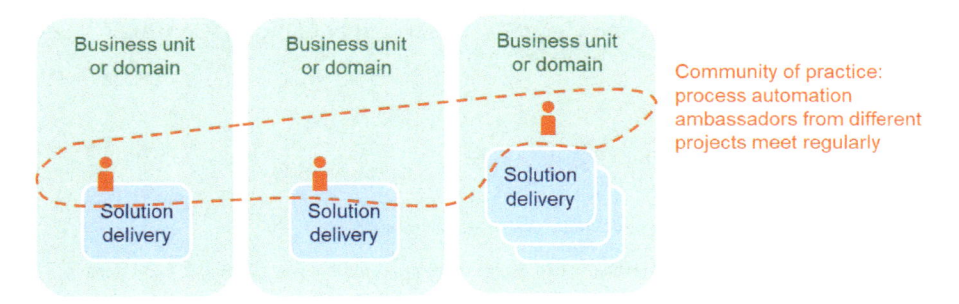

Figure 30: Fully decentralized delivery with CoP

Advantages:

- No central team is required, and no separate costs are involved.
- Very flexible.

Disadvantages:

- Inefficient due to lack of governance. Business units often end up with different approaches, which leads to a lot of challenges during the lifetime of solutions. This can become a severe obstacle to increasing automation in highly regulated environments such as banking and insurance.

- There is no ownership of the process orchestration topic, which means there is no single person responsible for fielding questions, managing vendor relationships, or taking part in industry events or conferences.

- Highly dependent on individuals' commitment and desire to exchange ideas. Often, a CoP boils down to a group of motivated individuals who drive the community in their "free time," which can potentially conflict with their daily responsibilities. An organization can address this by dedicating a set amount of time each week or month to the community, but still, this can create uncertainty because contributors often don't have a mandate to set up an enterprise strategy around process orchestration.

- There may be a lack of focus and commitment around the topic, since this is pretty much a bottom-up affair.

- Reuse is not facilitated, as nobody is responsible for providing reusable artifacts or investing the effort to make the project work (whether code or knowledge) reusable.

In essence, such a completely decentralized approach typically does not scale well. Still, it can be a good starting point to get a conversation about a CoE going.

In addition, it's important to note that a CoE and a CoP are not mutually exclusive. Best-of-breed organizations have both! For instance, at the National Bank of Canada, the CoE has actively built an internal community to share knowledge (as described at CamundaCon 2022[40]. See Figure 31).

Early days of the CoE: building governance

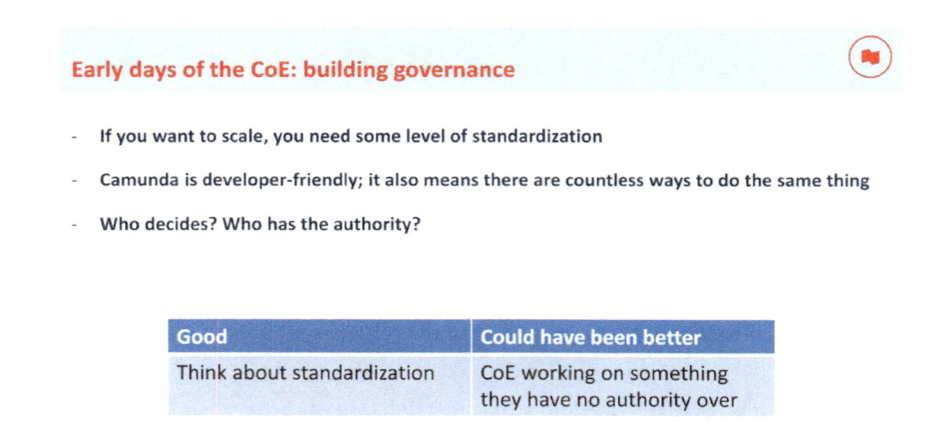

- If you want to scale, you need some level of standardization
- Camunda is developer-friendly; it also means there are countless ways to do the same thing
- Who decides? Who has the authority?

Good	Could have been better
Think about standardization	CoE working on something they have no authority over

Figure 31: Early days of National Bank of Canada's CoE (from CamundaCon 2022 presentation)

Fully Centralized Delivery

Next, let's look at the opposite side of the spectrum, where you can find more centralization if the CoE also implements and operates solutions itself. This means the business units are "only" required to capture the requirements; the CoE organizes everything else. It is almost like an internal solution integrator.

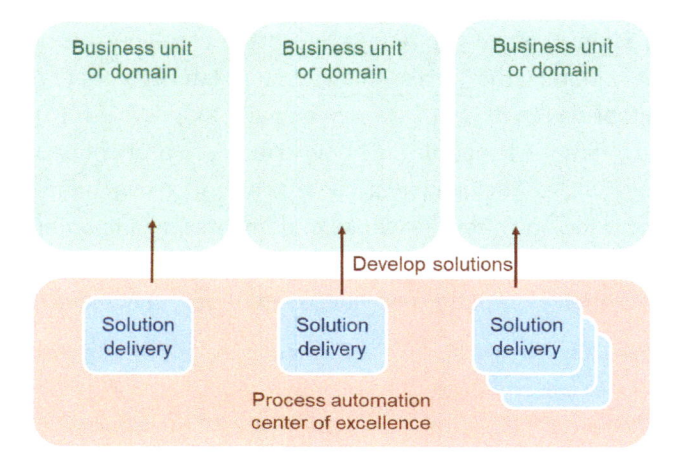

Figure 32: CoE responsible for solution delivery (fully centralized)

Advantages:

- The CoE is deep enough in the weeds to fully understand solution delivery and thus can give better recommendations.
- The CoE can not only control governance, but also the quality of the solutions.
- The CoE can make sure solutions are built in such a way that they can be easily operated.
- Business units without their own IT capacity have a shared services model to rely on.

Disadvantages:

- The CoE quickly becomes a bottleneck.
- The need for automation solutions in most organizations is so big that the CoE will need to grow into its own software engineering unit, probably losing its focus.
- The CoE lacks business domain expertise.
- The approach doesn't comply with state-of-the-art software development paradigms (as described in "How Software Is Being Built Today" starting on page 63).

In general, we advise against the CoE doing implementation work on a broad basis, as this simply conflicts too much with whatever software engineering function you already have. We prefer to keep a sharp focus in the CoE on enablement, letting business units do the implementation themselves or connecting them to partners (internally or externally) that can do it for them.

That said, there are exceptions when a CoE *should* actually be part of development. These include:

- **Early maturity stages:** When you're getting started with your process orchestration endeavors (if you remember the Process Orchestration Maturity Model[41] from "The Process Orchestration Adoption Framework" starting on page 12, this is level 1), you may simply not have the know-how yet to enable anybody. In fact, you probably won't have staffed a CoE yet either, but still, for the first few projects (say, one to five) it makes sense to have one team of people looking after the whole implementation, including go-live (relating to maturity level 2). This team of people might become your CoE when you move on to maturity level 3 or 4. This is a pattern we have seen be very successful in the past.

- **Strategic key projects:** When the organization is implementing important core processes with high complexity and significant top management attention, it may be strategically wise for the CoE to be part of the implementation project to ensure things don't go south, as that could damage the reputation of process orchestration and thus put the CoE in trouble.

- **Lighthouse projects:** When a new domain begins to use process orchestration, it may make sense for the CoE to be closely involved with the first few use cases. That way, the CoE can make sure the initiatives are delivered on time and on budget, as well as showcasing the potential value of process orchestration, which is very important for stakeholder acceptance. This involvement can facilitate knowledge transfer, and the CoE can gradually shift responsibility toward the domain.

- **Regular (re-)assessment of practices**: A CoE always bears the risk of living too much in the ivory tower. Therefore, it's vital to stay grounded in real-life implementation projects. While this can be done in a consulting role, it really helps to go into the trenches, at least occasionally.

Roles

Most organizations have similar roles with the same requirements and learning paths, even if the exact names of the job profiles might differ. We list the most common ones here.

Note that people working in a CoE should generally have an appetite for innovating. This does not necessarily mean they always want to use the latest and greatest technologies, but more that they want the organization to embrace change toward a better future. They must be willing to take some risks and embrace failure as an opportunity to learn and improve.

CoE Leader

The CoE leader manages the CoE, typically reporting to the CIO or a senior manager within the IT department. Sometimes, the CoE leader also reports to a senior program manager, e.g., around digital transformation. Ideally, there is C-level attention and clear communication to foster recognition of the CoE's impact on the overall goals of the organization.

A good CoE leader is enthusiastic about the opportunities of process orchestration and can help challenge the status quo in different parts of the organization by envisioning a better world with process orchestration. Therefore, this person should be pretty convincing, especially when talking to senior managers or conservative parts of the organization.

Goals:

- Enable the organization to successfully conduct all process automation initiatives.
- Support the overarching digital transformation process with adequate process automation technology.
- Demonstrate the success of these initiatives, mostly by looking at specific projects and their business outcomes.
- Create awareness of the potential of process orchestration in the different LoBs, thereby generating a flow of new initiatives.

Skills and requirements:

- Technical background, understanding of technology (and security)
- Able to speak "the language of the business," thereby linking technology to business potential
- Strategic thinking
- Communication and presentation skills
- Enthusiasm about process automation and the benefits it brings to the table, as this can be an uphill battle in some organizations

Enterprise Architect

Enterprise architects don't just look at IT architectures; they must understand the company's mission in sufficient detail to make informed purchases and architecture decisions across the enterprise. Enterprise architects commonly make high-level design choices on all things IT and propose technical standards, including coding standards, tools, or platforms.

For CoEs, it is important to keep in close touch with enterprise architects, as they typically pursue similar goals and have a similarly central role.

A well-respected enterprise architect could also be a great CoE leader.

Rainmaker

There is a very influential role that is often forgotten when looking at enterprise process orchestration, or more generally at adopting new technologies—we call this role the *rainmaker*, as that term conveys the idea of someone who can bring about positive outcomes, much like how rain brings growth to crops and prosperity to farmers. The rainmaker's job is to drive significant change or transformation through the successful implementation and adoption of new technologies. They may sit inside or outside the CoE, depending on the profile and influence of the person filling this role.

The rainmaker is often a visionary leader who has a deep understanding of both the organization's strategic objectives and the potential impact of technology on its operations. They are able to articulate a compelling vision for how technology can drive innovation, improve efficiency, and create competitive advantages for the organization. The rainmaker is adept at overcoming resistance to change by effectively communicating the benefits and addressing concerns or barriers to adoption.

In a nutshell, this person can make the business not only understand why adopting process orchestration is important, but also become enthusiastic about it. They help business departments to select orchestration candidates and can create a compelling business case for senior leadership out of any opportunity. They also are adept at communicating success and value to every executive level. Since the rainmaker is influential on both sides (business and IT), they can provide a link between the two and act as a translator.

Skills and requirements:

- Needs to have some technical knowledge to understand what process orchestration can do, but more important is that they understand the business processes, to see where orchestration can bring the most value
- Great networker, good at making connections
- Proficient at cross-functional collaboration across multiple domains and hierarchies
- Strong communicator; comfortable with business and IT jargon, understands what type of information is important to which people and is capable of presenting the right metrics to the right people

Business Analyst

The business analyst bridges the gap between non-technical stakeholders and IT people and translates the desired business logic of an application from business to technical language. They need to be able to communicate well with a variety of people while also being able to structure and prioritize very strictly (a combination many people struggle with). Responsibilities and tasks vary widely depending on the organization, but business analysis is important at all stages of the software system development lifecycle.

Business analysts should be involved in any process orchestration project. As business analysts are typically not required full-time on a project, they often look after multiple projects (or products) at the same time. Many CoEs also have their own business analysts, who either enable other business analysts to adopt a process mindset with BPMN or hop in and out of delivery projects to focus on business analysis there.

Skills and requirements:

- Analyzing, documenting, and managing requirements
- Converting vague bits and pieces into structured information
- Ability to communicate between business and IT
- Understanding processes and being able to use the modeling standards BPMN and DMN
- Tracking value and KPIs, e.g. in Camunda Optimize

Solution or IT Architect

Solution or IT architects design the general architecture of a solution, which also involves defining the tool stack and procedures being used (e.g., Camunda SaaS, CI/CD pipeline, issue tracking, etc.) and respective best practices. They're often instrumental at the beginning of a project, when the first lines of code are being written, but their role becomes less important once the focus shifts to implementing more of the same.

The role of solution architect is often played by senior developers or the solution delivery team as a whole—it's vital to success, but doesn't have to be filled by a dedicated person. The more standardized your development approach is, the more solution architecture is predefined by the CoE. In those cases, solution architects might also sit within the CoE. Often, we see CoEs deploying solution architects to guide the delivery teams in the LoBs throughout the project lifecycle.

Skills and requirements:

- Good overview of technological possibilities and their impact
- Good strategic overview of the lifetime of solutions
- Experience with different technical architectural styles

Software Developer

Not surprisingly, software developers develop software. They write well-tested and maintainable code to produce software according to business requirements. As part of this role they may leverage different frameworks and libraries, including a process orchestration platform. Software developers focused on process orchestration can sit within the CoE or the delivery teams.

Within the CoE, software developers typically concentrate on helping out with projects, consulting other developers, or developing and documenting reusable artifacts. These developers should have enthusiasm for process orchestration.

Within the delivery teams, software developers make process models executable, connect them to endpoints, and write proper tests. In order to be productive with an orchestration platform, they need to learn the basics of the process modeling language (e.g., BPMN) as well as gaining a solid foundation in core workflow engine concepts and APIs.

In *Practical Process Automation*[42], we differentiated "rockstars" and professional software developers. While rockstars can perform miracles, you typically don't have many of them in the organization, and these people also bear the risk of overengineering or applying the latest and greatest technologies just to avoid getting bored. Rockstars can be a help in your CoE, but take care that they don't push the CoE toward overengineering. Also, rockstars are sometimes not good at dealing with "normal" developers, meaning that coaching is not their strong point.

Skills and requirements:

- Software engineering background
- Understands how the process orchestration platform fits into the organization's IT architecture
- Embraces visual methods like BPMN (some developers are scared of visual models, for different reasons)

Low-Code Developer

Within the process automation space, you often hear about low-code developers. These may be trained software engineers who prefer to work in a low-code environment to simplify integration tasks and streamline the work, or they may have a business background and have slipped into development using tools like Microsoft Office, macros, or RPA.

Low-code developers often spend their time developing solutions in a dedicated low-code environment. They require a very constrained environment and a highly customized training course in the exact environment they will be working in.

For many companies, the key to scaling their process automation efforts is enabling these developers to model executable workflows. Low-code developers are typically part of the solution delivery teams, not part of the CoE itself. They may also be called business technologists, as this name reflects that they might work outside of IT departments.

Skills and requirements:

- Experience with BPMN
- Experience with low-code platforms

Note that low-code developers are not citizen developers. Citizen developers are typically end users with some IT affinity, not developers working on solutions all the time. Their aim is to solve an active pain point with a technology they can master. Solutions implemented by citizen developers are often outside the scope of the processes we cover in this book, but of course, there is a gray area in between.

Operations Engineer

Operations engineers look at running process solutions (or more generally, applications) in production environments from a technical point of view. Some operations engineers understand how to provision machines (e.g., Terraform, Kubernetes, etc.) and how to run software on them (e.g., Docker, Kubernetes, etc.). Others focus on technical operations, meaning they can monitor applications and resolve issues when they occur. They can work in the front row of support, relying on developers whenever a problem goes deeper into process or application specifics. Very often, operations engineers work on call to provide 24/7 support for critical applications. Consequently, they tend to look more for stability than fancy features and often provide a good balance in any delivery team.

If your CoE operates software, you will need at least two operations engineers. Working on call and providing sufficient support coverage is not feasible with fewer people, unless you weaken the business requirements around incident resolution times.

The CoE might also have at least one operations engineer to consult with delivery teams and make sure that operational concerns are not left out of best practices.

Skills and requirements:

- Knows how to run software applications reliably
- Can read and understand technical logs
- Knows BPMN and process orchestration basics
- Able to collaborate with InfoSec teams to meet security standards (sometimes InfoSec experts can be provisionally part of the CoE, e.g. during the initial platform setup)

The Center of Excellence (CoE)

We've already discussed the importance of having a center of excellence in an organization, and we're seeing huge traction for this concept in our customer base and the overall market. This is reflected in the numbers. In our State of Process Automation 2020 report[43], 90% of participants indicated that they already had a CoE, were actively working on implementing one, or had it on their roadmap. The number of active CoEs has likely grown even higher today, given that in our State of Process Orchestration 2023 report[44], 96% of respondents stated they believe that process automation is critical to achieving their digital transformation goals.

There's a good reason for this: a CoE is a game changer if you truly want to transform your business through process orchestration. To put it bluntly, **if you want to scale process automation, you need to establish a center of excellence.**

So, let's dive deeper into what a CoE for process orchestration is and how to set it up.

What Is a CoE for Process Orchestration?

A CoE for process orchestration is a dedicated team of experts that drives a strategic, scaled adoption of process orchestration across the enterprise. This definition is deliberately open because the exact setup of a CoE varies wildly depending on the goals, enterprise architecture, and culture of the respective organization. Generally, we can say that the goal is to make the adoption of process orchestration as frictionless as possible by providing the necessary tools, building the corresponding automation skills, delivering value through automation initiatives, and creating awareness for the topic.

The CoE does not have to be referred to within the organization as a "center of excellence"; we have seen many different names for it, including "competence center," "capability center," "digital enabler," "process automation guild," and more. Regardless of the name, they all share the common goal of accelerating the successful use of process orchestration across the organization.

The Scope of Your CoE

Your CoE should at least own the process orchestration topic, with all its related facets; for instance, also advising on how integration is typically done, how humans are pulled into processes, and how executable processes can be automatically tested. As an example, Figure 33 illustrates how the CoE at Provinzial, Germany's second-biggest public insurance company, defined the typical specifications of a process model (e.g., service task, user task, and data warehouse integrations as well as DMN, modeling conventions, etc.).

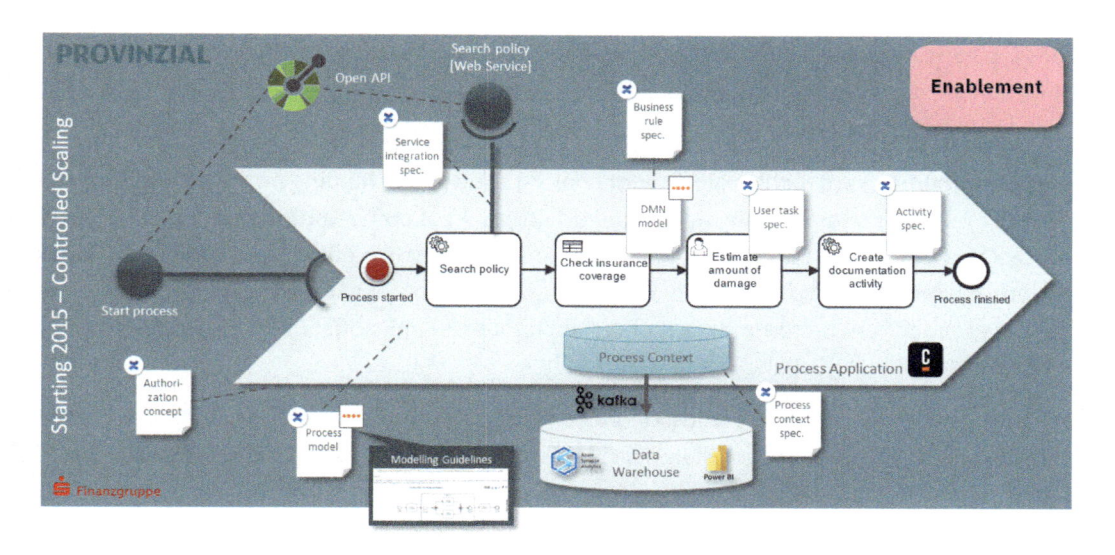

Figure 33: How to design an executable process at Provinzial, as defined by its CoE (taken from Provinzial's CamundaCon 2023 presentation)

Ideally, your CoE will look after all process automation technologies holistically, so in addition to process orchestration it will also be in charge of RPA tools, business process management suites, and low-code tools. For example, we saw one "process automation CoE" at a bigger customer looking after Camunda, Pega, UIPath, and Mendix. The big benefit of this is that the people in the CoE will understand the differences between those tools, as well as their respective sweet spots. The CoE will therefore be able to provide guidance on which tools and technologies to choose for specific use cases, which is much more beneficial than having two different competence centers being at war with each other. This way, the CoE can effectively drive vendor rationalization efforts as well. (That said, we have also seen customers benefit from having different CoEs for different tools, typically because a healthy friction between the approaches drives innovation.)

Take care not to widen the scope too much beyond process automation, however, as, for example, a "digital transformation CoE" can easily end up with too many topics and tools to look after to work effectively.

What About Communities of Practice (CoPs)?

A community of practice is "a group of people who share a common interest, passion, or profession and come together to learn from one another, share experiences, and collaborate on solving problems or advancing their collective knowledge and skills in a specific domain" (ChatGPT). Those communities often form organically within an organization, because individuals all working with process orchestration, for example, find each other. Like a CoE, a CoP does not have to be named "CoP"; we also see other names in use, like "interest group," "expert exchange," or "guild."

CoPs typically organize communication channels, like regular meetings or knowledge forums. While they may start out as something as simple as a wiki page, most CoPs we know of also run biweekly meetings and have a dedicated channel in Teams or Slack.

These communities are highly valuable for sharing knowledge, helping projects avoid making the same mistakes over and over again, and driving process orchestration maturity. But here's the catch: a CoP requires some organization, and typically there is no one individual who's responsible for this, and no official mandate or budget. In other words, the functioning of the CoP is dependent on the commitment of certain interested individuals, and if their priorities or duties shift, the whole CoP may be at risk.

This is why we advise having a dedicated role to organize the CoP. Not only is it a lot of work, but it also requires continuity and passion. The ideal place for such a task is the CoE. This also means that a CoE and CoP are not mutually exclusive. In fact, ideally they come as a pair.

What Should Your CoE Look Like?

CoEs can differ in many ways. They can be sizable teams with more than a dozen people, but we've also seen successful CoEs with only two people. It all boils down to your organization's size, your strategy, and what will help with your target operating model. That will determine the appropriate size, staffing, and activities for your CoE.

Let's first explore what a mature CoE will look like, before diving into the journey to build it. The setup that our customers with the highest level of process orchestration maturity deploy tends to look like this:

- A centralized team that helps delivery teams with all things process orchestration, comprising four to eight people filling the following roles:
- CoE lead
- Software developers
- IT/solution architects
- DevOps engineers
- Business analysts (BPMN & DMN experts)
- The rainmaker may also sit within the CoE, but more often than not they provide external support.
- The CoE team see themselves as enablers, and the organization pulls their offering. Delivery teams love to use their help because it makes their lives easier and their projects more successful.

- The CoE provides a set of artifacts (best practices, reusable components, and some templates) and a process orchestrations infrastructure (in the case of Camunda, for example, either a self-managed Camunda installation provided via self-service to the organization, or simply relaying the Camunda SaaS offering).

Delivery teams and CoEs can be augmented by other centralized IT resources or third-party partners (e.g., outsourcing operations). This is visualized in Figure 34.

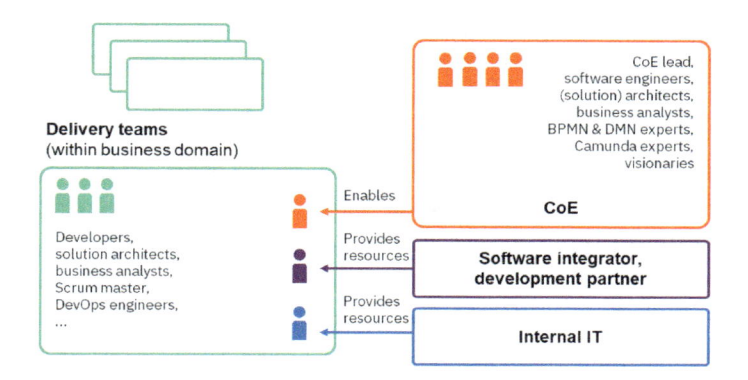

Figure 34: Delivery teams receive support and resources from the CoE and other internal and external actors.

The best CoEs we have seen have a product mindset (see "Product Thinking" starting on page 65). They view themselves as building an internal product, like a framework, tooling, or a platform, and they see developers, operations teams, SecOps, and other stakeholders as internal customers. So, just like product design software vendors do, they always source their ideas from those customers and validate their decisions with them, making it easy for customers to provide feedback or request functionality and making sure they know they will be listened to. Remember: you're building it *for* those folks, and not because you know better. A good reference here (although it focuses more on the platform side of the CoE) is the article "What I Talk About When I Talk About Platforms"[45] on Martin Fowler's blog.

The setup pictured in Figure 29 is our greenfield choice (remember: if there are no good reasons not to use the greenfield choice, we try to set things up this way). But as we mentioned earlier, reality is complex, so there might be good reasons to use a different setup in your organization. For example, some company cultures are built around strong rules and enforcement, so it would alienate employees if the CoE were just sitting there waiting for people to ask for help. Still, it's helpful to keep this greenfield recommendation in mind and make deliberate choices about where to deviate from it.

The Business Case for the CoE

In our experience, the higher up a CoE reports in an organization, the more effective it can be. In that sense, it's mandatory to get management buy-in and sufficient funding for your CoE initiative. That's why articulating the associated business impact is crucial. There are two dimensions to this:

1. Why process automation and process orchestration?
2. Why a center of excellence?

In other words, you have to make a case for what you want to do (process orchestration) first, before you can argue why the CoE will make you more successful in adopting it.

In general, the CoE will help you harvest the value proposition of process orchestration at scale in your organization. This is less about *what* you achieve through successful orchestration initiatives (for example, improved process cycle times) and more about *how* those initiatives are being delivered. A CoE will help teams to become more efficient and agile, while also improving the (internal) customer experience for your developer community (e.g., by helping them reduce their mental load through the technical advantages provided by the CoE). But of course, the CoE can also help in finding the right opportunities and business cases for process orchestration and expressing their value.

The strategic impact of the CoE on the business is unfortunately tough to quantify, as there are a lot of factors that contribute to it. On the other hand, simple metrics around the number of people trained in process orchestration or the level of adoption within the organization hint at the value a CoE is delivering but are not directly connected to its business impact; they are only what is known as proxy metrics. This trade-off is illustrated by the CoE value pyramid in Figure 35, which we adapted from the paper "Managing Value in Use in Business Markets"[46] by business researchers Michael Kleinaltenkamp and Katharina Prohl.

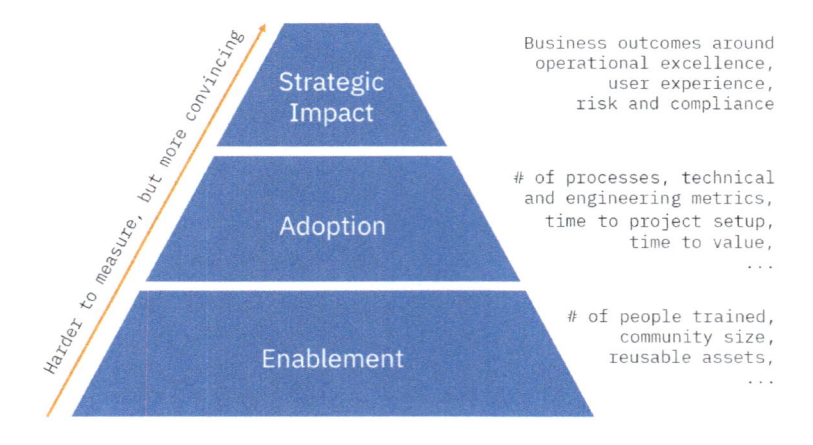

Figure 35: The CoE value pyramid

In general, successful CoEs are better at communicating their value at higher levels of the pyramid and translating this into business outcomes. In order to help you do this, let's dive into the concrete advantages that a CoE provides. Foremost among these are:

- **Increased developer productivity:** Having a CoE that takes care of best practices, project templates, getting started guides, governance, and other materials will drastically improve the productivity of delivery teams. Just think of the time and effort required to start an automation initiative from scratch: evaluating a tool, deciding on an architecture and approach, burning your fingers with the first mistakes you make, etc. In our experience, it can take teams two to six months to go through this cycle, which a CoE can significantly accelerate. As Deepak Tiwari, Managing Director at EY, put it in one of our blog posts[47]: "CoEs usually have visibility across other projects across the organization. They may have seen pitfalls the delivery team may not have been exposed to (better to learn from others' mistakes than your own)." Beyond knowledge sharing, CoEs might also provide technical accelerators such as connectors or an internally managed platform to reduce the cognitive load for delivery teams. We will discuss this later in more detail.

- **Efficiency and cost savings:** Of course, increased efficiency of your development teams will save effort and thus make completing projects quicker and cheaper. While this will typically not lead to a reduced headcount (after all, we're still facing a talent shortage), it means that you can improve your developer productivity and automate more within your existing setup, leading to further efficiencies and cost savings. A CoE can, for example, also make sure that licenses for tools are efficiently used and standardized, helping with the process of vendor rationalization.

- **Improved quality and reduced complexity:** Documenting best practices and making sure there is knowledge exchange between teams will result in teams consistently producing higher-quality (for example, more maintainable) solutions and delivering results on budget and on time. A CoE will also help provide the right technology, thereby allowing a best-of-breed approach and reducing complexity for agile delivery teams. Just looking at the sheer size of the CNCF Cloud Native Landscape[48] illustrates the challenges that delivery teams face here—how are they supposed to keep track of all the different tools? A CoE helps improve time to value significantly by shaving off the evaluation time for the respective teams. Additionally, the CoE can help avoid obscure or suboptimal technology choices made by inexperienced teams or playful individuals that will cause maintenance efforts later on.

- **Process mindset and stakeholder enablement:** Typically, the adoption of process orchestration at scale corresponds with a wider transformation of how an organization thinks about processes and how business and IT teams collaborate. As a survey by McKinsey[49] pointed out in 2022, the more parts of the organization are involved, the more automation initiatives are likely to succeed. CoEs can help build this process mindset by providing the right tools and frameworks to enable every stakeholder, including citizen developers, to take part in process orchestration—from modeling to development, operation, analysis, and continuous improvement. It can also encourage stakeholder buy-in and provide strategic alignment across domains and hierarchies by building a mutual vision of what to achieve through process orchestration.

In summary, as an IT executive at one of our customers put it: "Process orchestration allows us to create solutions more quickly, making the resulting systems more reliable, and the CoE ensures the organization is leveraging all of that in the best way possible."

Building Your CoE

To formally set up a CoE and maximize its impact on your organization, you will need management buy-in and sufficient funding. This typically happens either through a buildup of enough bottom-up pressure (i.e., more and more teams articulating the desire to use process orchestration) or through a strategic top-down initiative to drive process orchestration at scale.

In the previously mentioned blog post[50], Deepak Tiwari also excellently summarizes how to get management buy-in for funding a CoE:

1. **Think "big"** (and make the stakeholders think big). Show the "big picture"—[describe] strategic benefits, visualize your target operating model, paint a clear picture of the future state and an implementation roadmap to get there.

2. **Start small**. Ask for small funding in the beginning. A 90-day go-live plan is a good idea. Pick a high-value but low-effort use case for a pilot "lighthouse" project. Get a meaningful win that will help consolidate business sponsorship and build momentum.

3. **Finish strong**. Maintain executive sponsorship and commitment throughout the duration of the program by focusing on benefits realization.

After those phases, Deepak suggests **scaling** and **continuously improving** your CoE. We typically use the following four phases to describe building a CoE, as visualized in Figure 36:

- **Initial:** Organizations that are just getting started with adopting process orchestration don't have a CoE yet. There might be a CoP established to facilitate knowledge sharing and start the journey toward a CoE, or a strategic plan to scale process orchestration and create a CoE.

- **Forming:** The CoE starts to exist as a dedicated team within the organization and begins developing guidelines and infrastructure. It either focuses on enabling from the beginning or is deeply involved in the first solution delivery projects itself.

- **Scaling:** Now it's time to scale the adoption across the enterprise and evolve the CoE accordingly. Experience from more and more projects improves the maturity and credibility of the CoE. The CoE needs to improve at capturing metrics and communicate the business value of process automation and of itself to secure funding. Typically, in this phase we see stronger centralization of governance, enablement, and infrastructure and increasingly federated delivery in the business domains.

- **Maturing:** The CoE is established and helps with the strategic application of process automation and orchestration throughout the organization. It's continuously improving its offering across the board.

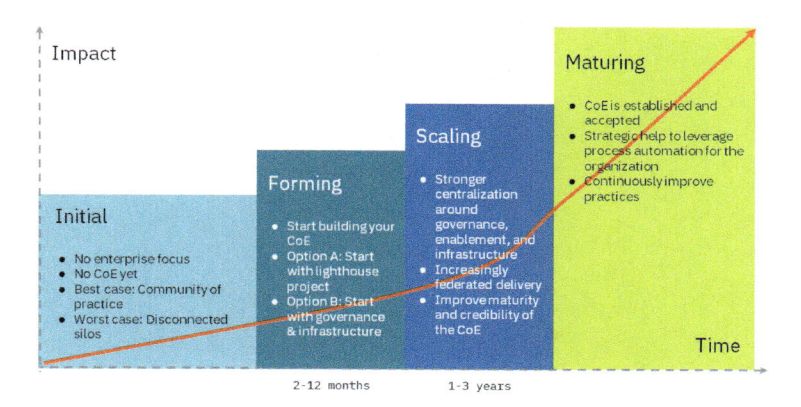

Figure 36: The four phases of building a CoE

Keep in mind that this is an iterative journey and you need to get there step by step, focusing on incrementally delivering value, ideally from day one.

CoE Tasks

Now let's dive a bit more deeply into how a CoE provides its value. What activities does a CoE normally perform, and which activities is it better to avoid? Let's start by going over the core activities of a CoE, including the typical resources a CoE provides (Figure 37).

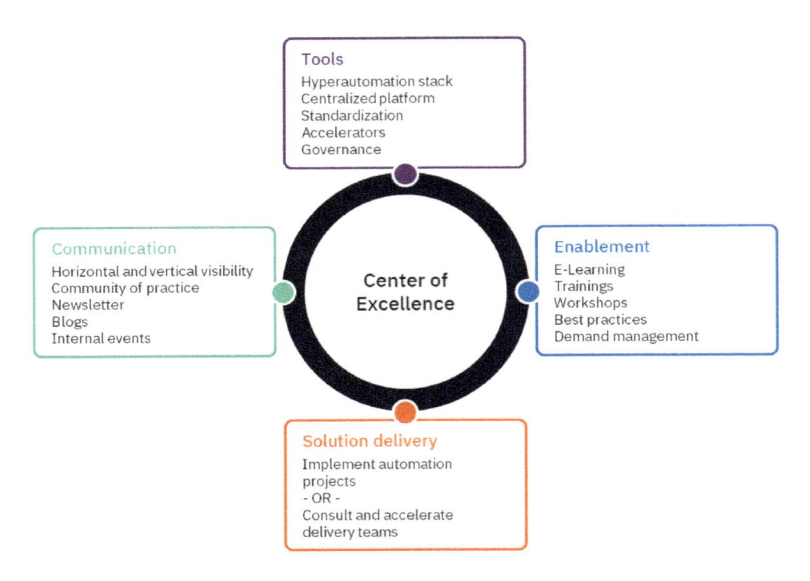

Figure 37: The core activities of a CoE

We've grouped the tasks into four main categories: enablement, communication, tools, and solution delivery. Let's go over these one by one.

Communication

A CoE needs to **evangelize process automation**. This can be done in many ways. You can hold **internal events** like lunch and learn[51] meetings, tech days, success story presentations, vendor pitches, or roadmap discussions, many of which your process orchestration vendor can also support. Also, hackathons are a great way to spread the word in a fun and engaging way. And don't forget about the power of **good branding**, perhaps coming up with something a bit more fun than a "process orchestration CoE." At one customer, we saw "Process Samurai" stickers on various laptops throughout the firm, and others had their own great T-shirts. Keep in mind that the branding should fit your company's culture (at Camunda, humor always works well!).

Additionally, you can leverage **external events** like industry conferences or vendor events (for example CamundaCon[52], Camunda days[53], or regional meetups[54]). Surprisingly enough, good external presentations often get more internal attention than internal events. We frequently connect different business units within a single customer that don't yet know each other through Camunda events.

Apart from events, you can write about your experiences. **Case studies** are a good way to communicate value, and many CoEs write extensive internal case studies for all projects. Emphasize the benefits and point to quick wins. The better you are able to **quantify the achieved value**, the more convincing those case studies will be. You can also participate in vendor case studies (e.g., Camunda case studies[55]), typically revealing fewer details but getting more exposure. Also, most CoEs run a regular **newsletter** or maintain a news section in their wiki that people can subscribe to.

The CoE should also try to **foster internal communication**. By hosting regular coffee meetings, reviews, open spaces, or other kinds of workshops, the CoE can give the impression of being approachable and caring.

Part of this is also to make sure the right technical foundation is in place to form and **manage a community of practice**, where all professionals involved with process automation can easily meet and exchange ideas. Typically, companies provide a **forum** or **Slack channel**, a **blog** or **wiki** section, or regular speaking slots at company-wide meetings.

CoEs typically also **manage vendor contacts and licenses** (together with their procurement, of course). Centralizing this not only makes collaboration with vendors more efficient, but can also help ensure the right configurations of the tools are applied and licensing is optimized for all use cases. For instance, Camunda allows licenses to grow without going through a complete sales and legal cycle every time, e.g., with agreed adoption paths or frame agreements.

We want to emphasize that good vendor support is vital for organizations to succeed, so vendor management is actually a more essential activity than most anticipate. A thorough understanding of the vendor's offering—not only with respect to features, but also customer success, support, and enabling services, as well as the vision and roadmap—is crucial for effectively improving your level of process orchestration maturity.

Enablement

The main goal of a CoE is to enable others in the organization to successfully implement process orchestration solutions. This can happen on many levels:

- **Consulting:** The CoE can be the go-to place to ask questions about process automation in general, methods like BPMN or DMN, or specific tools like Camunda. In a minimal form, the CoE is just **approachable for questions**. In a more structured way, this could include offering defined **consulting packages**: anything from a virtual coffee chat for projects thinking about using process orchestration or a half-day orientation **workshop** up to a five-day POC session. Many CoEs also stay close to projects, e.g. by conducting regular, proactive **check-ins** or **reviews**. In mature organizations we often see a quite broad offering, which to some extent reminds us of our consulting offerings, including out-of-the-box **training courses**.

    Instead of relying on rigid rules stating that people have to attend mandatory training courses, try to **build a learning culture**, where learning and training are seen as not only valuable and helpful, but also fun.

Note that it might also make sense to include vendor offerings (e.g., in-person training, or free **e-learning courses** from Camunda Academy[56]) in your own offering. In this case, the added value of the CoE is often in curating the important content and establishing a link between the vendor's generic world and the organization's specifics. This also results in a much more realistic workload, as it is hard for a CoE to develop and maintain too much material on its own.

- **Best practices:** Successful CoEs document their best practices, at least in a basic way. You might find some inspiration in the Camunda Best Practices[57], but the advantage a CoE has is that it can tailor the best practices to the organization, eliminating choices that aren't relevant. A good example of this is the solution architecture for automation projects, where it might be sufficient to define one common architecture for pro-code and another for low-code environments. This architecture can then include company specifics like which version control system is used, how a project can be hooked into CI/CD, and so on. (You don't need to call these best practices; it can simply be your process orchestration **documentation**.)

  CoEs might share those best practices in a **knowledge base**, capturing frequently answered questions (**FAQs**). This might simply happen in your company's wiki (e.g., Confluence), but of course, you can also use an internal forum or specific tools if there is enough internal traffic.

- **Demand management:** One big challenge in organizations is determining which projects will benefit from process orchestration. This includes identifying the candidate projects, describing the role process orchestration will play, budgeting, developing a business case presentation, defining KPIs, and finally prioritizing and planning those projects. The CoE can play an instrumental role in the whole process to support business initiatives with the insights required. Many CoEs have a low-touch entry point for initiatives to get in touch (one of our customers calls this the "Front Door"). Projects are then quickly assessed (for example, by a virtual coffee chat and templates to capture the important information), and recommendations can be given. The CoE can give an indication of whether or not process orchestration might be helpful in this project, and if so help show the value it can bring. It can also help to define the required roles to develop a solution and perhaps recommend development partners (both internal and external).

  CoEs in more mature organizations even start one step earlier and sit down with leaders of their business domains to proactively think about the potential of process orchestration for various use cases. Done well, this can reveal big **strategic opportunities** to **save money**, **earn more money**, or **reduce risk** through the benefits process orchestration brings to solution delivery.

Tools and infrastructure

As part of the enablement practice, or in addition to it, many CoEs provide guidance on the tool stack or additional reusable artifacts. Increasingly, CoEs provide a shared platform for process orchestration. This might involve defining any or all of the following:

The hyperautomation stack: A process automation CoE typically owns the full hyperautomation technology stack[58]. This means the CoE knows about a variety of tools from different categories and can give recommendations on which tool to use for a specific use case (we've sketched out a decision map for this in "Selecting the Right Process Orchestration Technology" starting on page 137). Typically, the CoE also has knowledge of how to combine those different tools, because, for example, you might want to orchestrate the overall end-to-end process with Camunda but integrate certain legacy systems via RPA within single tasks[59].

In most organizations, CoEs **recommend and provide specific tools** to be used. Depending on your organization's culture, this recommendation may be seen as a suggestion that can be ignored, or as an official standard that everybody has to follow. In addition, the CoE can **recommend the way tools should be used** in projects—for example:

- SaaS vs. self-managed
- The programming language used (e.g., Java and Spring Boot)
- How tests should be done (e.g., unit testing with JUnit, behavior-driven testing with Cucumber, integration testing with Selenium, etc.)
- The CI/CD pipeline (e.g., with Jenkins or GitHub Actions)

This can go even further. For example, we've seen CoEs that run **architecture workshops** and **architecture reviews**, and others that help projects that need high scale to do **load tests, benchmarks, or performance tuning**. In particular, activities that require deep expertise around a tool but are often unrelated to the business problem can be best supported by a CoE.

Accelerators: If the tool stack is standardized, the CoE can provide resources to make delivery teams more productive. There are many things that are quite similar in various projects, and in these cases it's simply easier to reuse the existing know-how and code. Good examples are:

- Project templates (e.g., a Maven Archetype or simply a template project to be copied)
- Frameworks that help with harmonization or standardization (e.g., build tools, Maven parent POMs, Maven BOMs, etc.)
- Installation scripts
- Connectors, including company-specific connectors for common systems (e.g., Mainframe or some bespoke core business system) or sometimes just reusable job workers and element templates
- Security configuration (e.g., SSO or LDAP integration and configuration)

- Plugins (e.g., for pushing audit data of the orchestration platform into the data warehouse)
- BPMN patterns for typical problems (e.g., maker-checker)

One specific form of accelerator is **internal marketplaces or portals**, which can be used as catalogs to find and leverage reusable artifacts—something that tends to become a big problem once adoption is scaled. While many CoEs in the past organized this via wikis, some have their own portal software (e.g., API portals). Camunda also provides a marketplace component that can be leveraged for this, as well as for sharing artifacts only internally. Such an internal marketplace would most likely be curated by the CoE and augmented by the contributions of the internal community.

Solution lifecycle: Many CoEs define what the solution lifecycle should look like. This might depend on the type of solution (pro-code vs. low-code), but typically, it aligns process development with the general **software development lifecycle (SDLC)**. So, for example, the CoE recommends how to version control your sources (e.g., using GitHub), what stages deployments should go through (e.g., DEV, INT, PRE-PROD, and PROD), how to deploy process models to production (e.g., with the BPMN being part of the deployment artifact deployed during startup), and what the CI/CD pipeline should look like (e.g., predefined GitHub Actions).

As part of the solution lifecycle, some organizations also establish **quality gates** or **approvals**. For example, a BPMN process model requires a review by the CoE before it can go live, or there may be a definition of done (DoD) that includes specific process-related checkpoints (e.g., that there is basic test coverage).

KPIs/value tracking: The CoE can support projects in identifying useful key performance indicators. In our experience, many project teams are unsure of which KPIs they should track and how to connect those to business goals. However, doing this is essential to prove the business value of process orchestration, identify bottlenecks and improvement opportunities, and track continuous improvements over time. The experts within the CoE can provide assistance with this.

Solution delivery

A CoE can also be involved with certain aspects of solution delivery, such as:

- **Evaluating the automation pipeline:** Organizations need to decide which projects process orchestration will be beneficial for and **prioritize** those projects so that (typically rare) resources can be distributed properly. The CoE can not only consult with the initiative stakeholders on the benefits of process orchestration and help with early estimations to make the business case, but often also **see opportunities** others have missed because they are not as familiar with process orchestration. For example, the CoE knows that you can easily change processes running on the orchestration platform later and that this will enable experiments with new technologies like AI.

- **Orchestrating partners:** The CoE can **coordinate with external partners** (software integrators, consulting companies, training providers) to **staff projects** or to find enablement support. Many CoEs work with a curated set of people at dedicated partners who they know are familiar with not only process orchestration and the tool being used, but also the specific needs of the organization. Of course, this can also work the same way with internal people, especially in bigger organizations.

- **Implementing automation projects:** Some CoEs also do real implementation work themselves. As discussed earlier, we generally advise against CoEs doing implementation work on a broad basis, but there are valid reasons for exceptions (see "Fully Centralized Delivery" starting on page 75).

Governance

Finding a healthy level of governance is not easy and requires balancing contradicting requirements. Forces advocating for more centralized governance in the context of process orchestration typically include:

- **Standardization and consistency:** Centralized governance allows for the establishment and enforcement of standardized processes, coding conventions, and best practices across the organization. This ensures consistency in software development, making it easier to maintain and manage codebases.

- **Security and compliance:** Centralized governance allows organizations to enforce security policies and data protection measures as well as to ensure compliance with industry standards and regulations.

- **Quality assurance:** With centralized governance, there can be a focus on quality assurance processes, including code reviews, testing standards, and quality metrics. This helps ensure that software products meet the required quality standards.

Forces advocating for more decentralized governance typically center around:

- **Agility and flexibility:** Decentralized governance allows for greater agility and flexibility in responding to changes and adapting to evolving requirements. Teams can make decisions independently and respond quickly to emerging opportunities or challenges without waiting for central approval.

- **Empowerment and autonomy:** Decentralized governance empowers teams by giving them autonomy over decision-making processes. It minimizes bureaucratic hurdles and eliminates the need for decisions to go through a centralized approval process. This can lead to increased motivation, creativity, and a sense of ownership among team members, fostering a more innovative and dynamic work environment.

- **Local expertise:** Decentralized governance allows decisions to be made by teams or individuals who possess local or specialized expertise. This is particularly beneficial when dealing with projects that require domain-specific knowledge or expertise that is distributed throughout the organization.
- **Innovation and experimentation:** Decentralized governance fosters a culture of innovation and experimentation. Teams can try out new ideas, technologies, or development methodologies without being constrained by rigid central guidelines, leading to more innovative solutions.

For most organizations it makes sense to aim for somewhere in the middle to get the best of both worlds, as we described in "A Healthy Level of Centralization" starting on page 69, with sweet spot being a central CoE that enables federated delivery teams and provides a platform, taking care to ensure the right level of governance in the platform and corresponding getting started guides, templates, and examples. For instance, most organizations provide a prebuilt integration into their single sign-on (SSO) environment, as this is crucial for every project and no creativity is required here. On the contrary, this should not become a hurdle and should just work out of the box. At the same time, the CoE might leave delivery teams the freedom to choose which libraries to use to connect their REST services.

In general, we are fans of the idea of golden paths[60]: using a solution template, for example, should be such a great experience that delivery teams will not see this as annoying bureaucracy, but as help they would never want to work without.

Of course, organizations are all different, so the approach to governance must be **aligned with your company culture**. For example, if your organization embraces microservices, heavily hyping the autonomy of development teams, any central guidance should be approached cautiously (while still ensuring that governance guardrails, however strictly or loosely they are designed, are respected). In contrast, if your organization is used to very rigid central governance, giving too much freedom to development teams might be a burden on those teams, which are not used to making their own decisions.

In summary, the path to getting to the sweet spot of governance might be very different for each organization.

Process Architecture and Process Landscapes

One topic that often comes up when discussing operating models and process orchestration maturity is *process architecture*. You can think of this as an overview of the processes in an organization. Typically it involves a high-level process landscape, where you will find all of the processes listed, often sorted by domains as well as by customer journeys. Some processes are also simply support processes. Others may be made up of other processes, and the process architecture tries to make this transparent too.

Process landscapes are done very differently in different organizations. Some try to gather a complete picture of the whole organization, often detached from IT implementation projects. Those landscapes are driven by dedicated functions that help to "organize" the organization. To be honest, their value is often limited and they are likely to be detached from reality. Other organizations take a much more pragmatic route to landscapes and create them as they go along their process orchestration journey, for example to help them pick automation candidates or to document what is already implemented.

It may be no surprise to you that we recommend the latter: a lightweight approach to sketch a simple map of processes in the organization. This does not necessarily require any sophisticated tooling, but can simply happen in your wiki.

Should your CoE drive this initiative? In general, we tend to say yes, but only if it's connected to real implementation projects. If your organization already creates a process landscape for documentation purposes alone, try to connect to those folks, but it's probably best not to get too involved in it.

CoE Anti-Patterns

As we all know, failure is the best teacher, but unfortunately those stories are seldom shared openly. So, we also want to describe some typical problems we've seen with our customers.

For instance, we saw one organization where the **delivery teams tried to avoid working with the CoE.** They developed autonomously and even procured their own licenses. The main reason cited was that **the CoE significantly slowed down delivery work** by adding bureaucracy and applying too-restrictive guidelines (e.g., mandatory quality checks that weren't helpful for the teams). In this case, the CoE was detached from the real challenges of delivery teams "on the ground" and created governance guidelines that were not only unhelpful but actually an obstacle—a typical ivory tower example.

To avoid this situation:

- **CoEs need to establish a continuous feedback loop** with all delivery initiatives (and potentially a CoP) to continuously evolve their offerings and align them with project needs. This is all about mindset. As mentioned previously, the CoE needs a product mindset and should be obsessed with providing value for the stakeholders in the organization.

- **The CoE model needs to evolve according to the needs of the organization**. While it might make sense to have stricter governance guidelines in the beginning, it might also make sense to provide more autonomy to enable scaling in later maturity stages (our customer Provinzial called this "managed autonomy" in their CamundaCon 2023 presentation[61]).

Another anti-pattern we've seen is **spending too much time on activities that don't have an impact** on the organization. This often comes up in a pair with "planning over doing" or "paralysis by analysis." The effect is that CoEs jeopardize their credibility, and people do not perceive them as valuable.

Instead, the CoE should:

- **Incrementally deliver value right away**. Of course, this should be done with a goal in mind, but the focus should be on going step by step and not getting bogged down by initiatives that only provide value after a significant amount of time has passed, with the risk of not being helpful at all in real life.
- **Adjust the plan** to accommodate any learnings along the way.

This plays into the next anti-pattern: **doing too much too early**. This can also be dangerous. For example, we have seen customers that wanted to build their own bespoke platform, provide lots of best practices around its usage, share reusable patterns, and so on. That all sounds good—but the problem was that they started when they didn't have any experience yet. Solution delivery teams, detached from the CoE, adopted the best practices early on, but they turned out not to work very well. This led to a lot of work being required within the CoE to fix problems or develop important features, very often in a firefighting manner, especially when the first project went live. After only a handful of projects, the team was completely blocked, ending up with a half-baked, relatively unstable platform and not enough capacity to enable projects.

Instead, the CoE should:

- **Harvest real learnings**, distill best practices, and **derive feature requests** for any software components they provide. The real-life context helps the CoE to provide meaningful artifacts.
- **Develop internal platforms incrementally** together with real-life projects.

Last but not least, we've seen CoEs struggle because they **lack a mandate** within the organization. This can lead to too little capacity to do impactful work and a shortage of credibility within the organization. To avoid this, it is crucial to **have sufficient authority and funding**. This is achieved by creating and sustaining stakeholder buy-in, especially with your internal sponsors. To that end, it is crucial to monitor and report on the business impact, not only to the sponsors, but also across the business, to generate interest in new initiatives.

Figure 38 shows a summary of some typical CoE anti-patterns and how to address them.

Challenge	Solution
✗ CoE detached from challenges of automation teams on the ground	✓ Continuous feedback loop with implementation teams and community of practice
✗ Provide too-restrictive guidelines and become added bureaucracy	✓ Focus on delivering value and adapt CoE model accordingly (e.g., shift responsibility to business domains, while providing useful accelerators and enablement)
✗ Spend too much time with initiatives that don't generate value (e.g., architecture frameworks)	✓ Promote an agile, iterative approach where you evolve and grow the CoE based on real-life use cases and challenges on the ground
✗ No management buy-in and backing in the company (leading to lack of authority & insufficient resources)	✓ Manage and align expectations with executive sponsor
✗ Lack of automation tools	✓ Provide wider automation toolset and leverage incumbent technology - there is no one size fits all
✗ Lack of success tracking	✓ Define desired outcomes and continuously monitor CoE impact on the global business
✗ Lack of visibility in the organization	✓ Showcase wins through case studies or events, such as a yearly "Automation day"

Figure 38: Common CoE challenges and how to solve them

Real-Life Examples

To give you a starting point to dive deeper into the topic, we want to give you some publicly disclosed examples of CoEs where more detailed information is available online:

- **NatWest**, a UK-focused banking organization, serving over 19 million customers, with business operations stretching across retail, commercial and private banking markets, has built a CoE that successfully scaled across the enterprise, with more than 4,000 Camunda users as of today. They talked about it at CamundaCon 2023[62].
- **National Bank of Canada** is the sixth-largest bank in Canada, with approximately 25,000 employees. Within this organization, a CoE of only two people has built and shared process automation expertise, set up a community of automation experts, and created standardization around the adoption of Camunda. They talked about it at CamundaCon 2022[63].
- **Provinzial**, a leading insurance company in Germany, has successfully adopted Camunda for end-to-end process orchestration across all domains, with over 220 processes and 270 decision tables in production. With their CoE, they are now advancing toward hyper-automation with AI integration. They talked about it at CamundaCon 2023[64].
- **Desjardins**, a Canadian financial service cooperative, set up a CoE to provide governance, enablement, and accelerators to use Camunda in their hyperautomation toolkit. They talked about it at CamundaCon 2022[65].

- **Goldman Sachs**, the multinational investment bank and financial services company, built an enterprise process automation platform on top of Camunda to enable automation at scale. You can read about why they built a platform on the Camunda blog[66] or listen to them talking about it at Camunda Community Summit 2022[67].

- The **City of Munich** ("Landeshauptstadt München") enables citizen development empowered by a Camunda-based workflow platform and a CoE in the IT department in order to boost the digital transformation of the administration in a scalable way. They talked about it at CamundaCon 2023[68].

- One of the largest commercial banks in Germany, Norddeutsche Landesbank (**NORD/LB**), set up a CoE to drive the adoption of process orchestration at the enterprise level. They talked about it in a process automation forum[69] (unfortunately, in German only).

Defining Your Target Operating Model

Defining the right target operating model is key for successful adoption of enterprise process orchestration. This model encompasses the team structure, processes, and capabilities that an organization aims to achieve to effectively deliver process orchestration solutions. While the target operating model also includes other aspects than people, like workflows and tools, we see the people-related aspects as the most important, which is why we're talking about it in this chapter.

Key Dimensions to Define Your Operating Model

Based on our discussions of the target operating model with many customers and prospects over the years, we've derived a set of eight dimensions you can use to evaluate the current state of your operating model, and define your target state:

- **Solution delivery:** What solution delivery model is used in your organization? Does your CoE provide some form of centralized enablement for building solutions? Do teams need to request it actively or is it provided broadly? Alternatively, is the CoE building solutions itself?

- **Enabling function (CoE):** Does your organization have an enabling function like a CoE? If so, what's the scope of the CoE? Is it focused on a single tool (e.g. Camunda), a wider category of tools (e.g., process orchestration), or some even broader topic (e.g., digital transformation in general)?

- **Infrastructure:** Does the CoE provide infrastructure (for example, add-ons or Camunda Connectors) instead of simply recommending a tool? Does it operate software and offer it via an internal SaaS model? Maybe it even provides the infrastructure to build, deploy, and run complete solutions.

- **Governance:** Is the CoE seen as an enabler that helps with projects or as a police force that mostly enforces guardrails? Are stacks standardized and obligatory, or documented as best practices you can choose to follow or not?

- **Process overview and value tracking:** Is your CoE the go-to place in the organization to gather an overview of business processes, probably providing some kind of process architecture or process landscape? Does it manage the automation backlog and proactively measure the value of automated processes within the business domains? Or are these the responsibilities of the business domains or another centralized unit?

- **Supported use case complexity:** Does the CoE focus on your core business processes that typically have a high degree of complexity and criticality and deliver a lot of value? Does it focus on the long tail of simpler processes that can potentially be implemented by citizen developers? Or does it cover the whole diverse set of processes, enabling it to see the sweet spots of the different tools being used?

- **Depth of enablement:** Does your CoE offer best practices, workshops, and training? Does it provide a specific learning and upskilling path for your organization?

- **Communication:** How much does your CoE invest in communication to create awareness about process orchestration? For example, does it work to build an internal community, do internal case studies and presentations, or even create sophisticated marketing materials?

Figure 39 provides an overview over those dimensions (you can access this graphic as a Google Slide[70] to visualize your own CoE design easily).

Solution delivery	Federated without central enablement	Internal consulting upon request	Internal enablement	Central implementation
Enabling function	None	Tool-specific CoE (e.g., Camunda)	CoE for wider category (e.g., process automation)	Very wide CoE (e.g., digitalization)
Provided infrastructure	Nothing	Project templates	Add-ons Hosted platform	Solution operations
Governance	Nothing		Recommendations (pull effect)	Standardized with obligation to follow (push)
Process overview & value tracking	No business process overview			Central process landscape and process architecture
Supported use case complexity	Core processes			Long tail of simple processes
Depth of enablement	Nothing (or outsourced)	Guides and best practices	Workshops and trainings	Learning and upskilling path
Communication	No proactive communication		Building an internal community	Sophisticated internal marketing

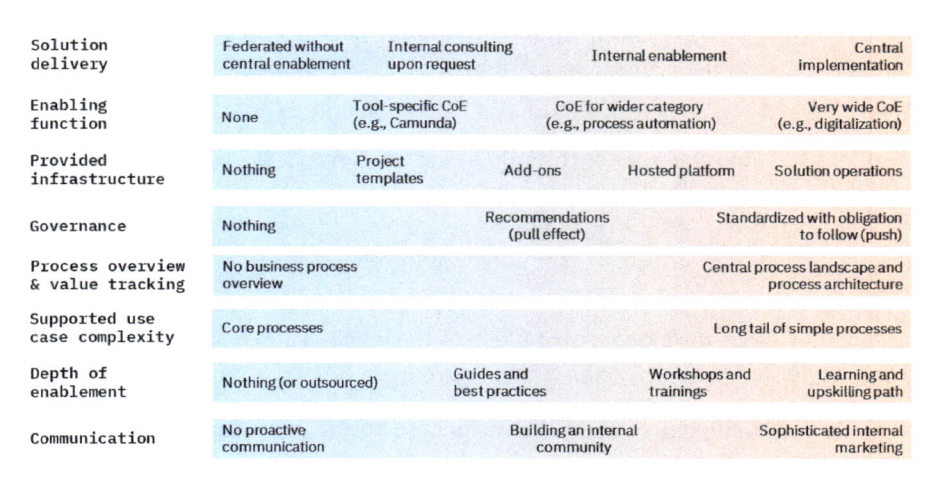

Figure 39: The target operating model dimensions

Considering these dimensions can be a big help in making key decisions around your target operating model. For example, our greenfield recommendation looks like Figure 40, where the green dots indicate the target state for each dimension.

Solution delivery	Federated without central enablement	Internal consulting upon request	Internal enablement ●	Central implementation
Enabling function	None	Tool-specific CoE (e.g., Camunda)	CoE for wider category ● (e.g., process automation)	Very wide CoE (e.g., digitalization)
Provided infrastructure	Nothing	Project templates	Add-ons	Hosted platform ● Solution operations
Governance	Nothing		Recommendations (pull effect) ●	Standardized with obligation to follow (push)
Process overview & value tracking	No business process overview		●	Central process landscape and process architecture
Supported use case complexity	Core processes			● Long tail of simple processes
Depth of enablement	Nothing (or outsourced)	Guides and best practices	Workshops and trainings	Learning and ● upskilling path
Communication	No proactive communication		Building an internal community ●	Sophisticated internal marketing

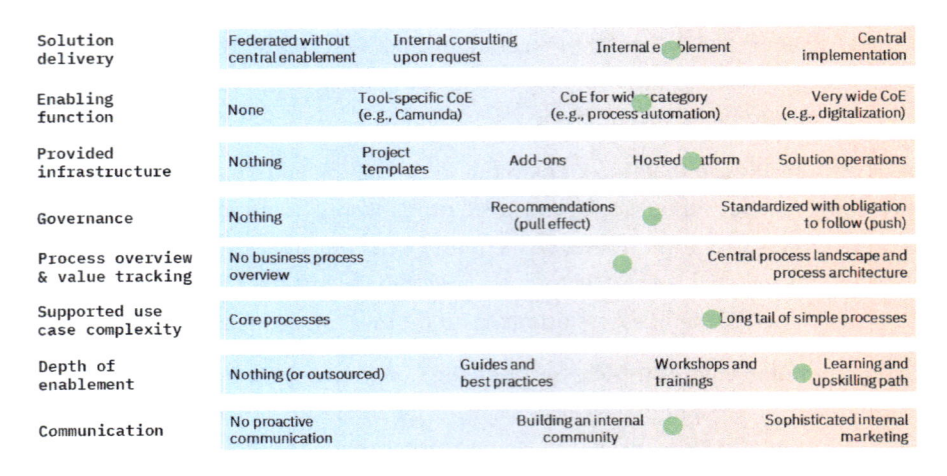

Figure 40: Our greenfield target operating model

This setup describes a CoE that:

- Fosters deep and strategic internal enablement, but does not implement solutions itself
- Provides a wide array of process automation tools, including a platform like Camunda, testing tools, RPA tools, and more
- Proactively guides delivery teams in their adoption of process orchestration (depending on the needs and skills of those teams)
- Hosts a centralized process orchestration platform as an internal SaaS offering, which is augmented by accelerators (e.g., integrations into the data warehouse, user task management, SSO, etc.)
- Provides sensible governance through a helpful reference architecture that matches the requirements of the internal teams
- Encourages process remodeling and value tracking to improve and measure the achieved value
- Enables low-code developers to implement the long tail of use cases with low or medium complexity
- Provides a training curriculum that is tailored to the organization's needs, leveraging internal and external resources
- Has built a strong internal community from which it learns while also continuously showcasing successes to the wider organization (business and management stakeholders)

Clarifying the target dimensions will help you set up your CoE. Things you'll want to consider:

- **Vision and mission statement:** Paint a target picture of your CoE to get internal buy-in.

- **Roadmap:** Build an action plan to bring the vision to life.
- **Staffing:** How many people will be in your CoE, and what are their roles and responsibilities? (The more centralized activities you have, the more personnel you need in your CoE.)
- **Operating model:** Will the CoE be run centrally for the whole organization, federated within business units or domains, or some hybrid in between?

Sketching Your Journey

The operating model dimensions are a wonderful tool to not only discuss the status quo of your organization, but also sketch out your journey.

For example, if you're facing a situation where there are a handful of different grassroots initiatives in place, resulting in different teams using process orchestration technology operating in fragmented silos without central ownership, you might want to start by identifying a central process orchestration **owner or champion**. This should be someone who has been involved in prior process orchestration projects. Most often, they are already widely regarded as an expert and informally consulted with technical questions. This person doesn't have a formal mandate and is typically driven by personal motivation, so the champion is actually not formally designated but informally grows into that role. This can be a great incubator for setting up a CoE.

This champion can build a **community of practice**. Building a CoP will help you bring together different users in the organization so they can learn from each other's projects. It will also help create visibility within the organization, showcasing successes and generating a snowball effect where success breeds success. That way, you can start to make an impression on the enterprise level, even if you don't yet have a formal mandate or budget for a CoE.

We often see the CoP as an interim solution for organizations where a CoE does not have funding yet but there are motivated individuals who want to push process orchestration forward, probably working toward making the case for a CoE.

You can see this stage visualized in Figure 41.

Solution delivery	Federated without central enablement	Internal consulting upon request	Internal enablement	Central implementation
Enabling function	None	Tool-specific CoE (e.g., Camunda)	CoE for wider category (e.g., process automation)	Very wide CoE (e.g., digitalization)
Provided infrastructure	Nothing	Project templates	Add-ons	Hosted platform	Solution operations
Governance	Nothing		Recommendations (pull effect)		Standardized with obligation to follow (push)
Process overview & value tracking	No business process overview			Central process landscape and process architecture
Supported use case complexity	Core processes			Long tail of simple processes
Depth of enablement	Nothing (or outsourced)	Guides and best practices	Workshops and trainings	Learning and upskilling path
Communication	No proactive communication		Building an internal community	Sophisticated internal marketing

Figure 41: The operating model of an organization that has not yet established a CoE

The advantages of process orchestration are proven with those first projects, but new projects cannot easily benefit from earlier experiences, despite informal conversations among community members.

This is an ideal breeding ground to form your CoE, often staffed with people who were part of the initial solution delivery teams. The CoE concentrates on enablement and governance and will probably not be part of new solution delivery projects. We see typical team sizes of two to eight people at this stage.

Plotted along our eight dimensions, the operating model during this formation stage looks like Figure 42.

Solution delivery	Federated without central enablement	Internal consulting upon request	Internal enablement	Central implementation
Enabling function	None	Tool-specific CoE (e.g., Camunda)	CoE for wider category (e.g., process automation)	Very wide CoE (e.g., digitalization)
Provided infrastructure	Nothing	Project templates	Add-ons	Hosted platform	Solution operations
Governance	Nothing		Recommendations (pull effect)		Standardized with obligation to follow (push)
Process overview & value tracking	No business process overview			Central process landscape and process architecture
Supported use case complexity	Core processes			Long tail of simple processes
Depth of enablement	Nothing (or outsourced)	Guides and best practices	Workshops and trainings	Learning and upskilling path
Communication	No proactive communication		Building an internal community	Sophisticated internal marketing

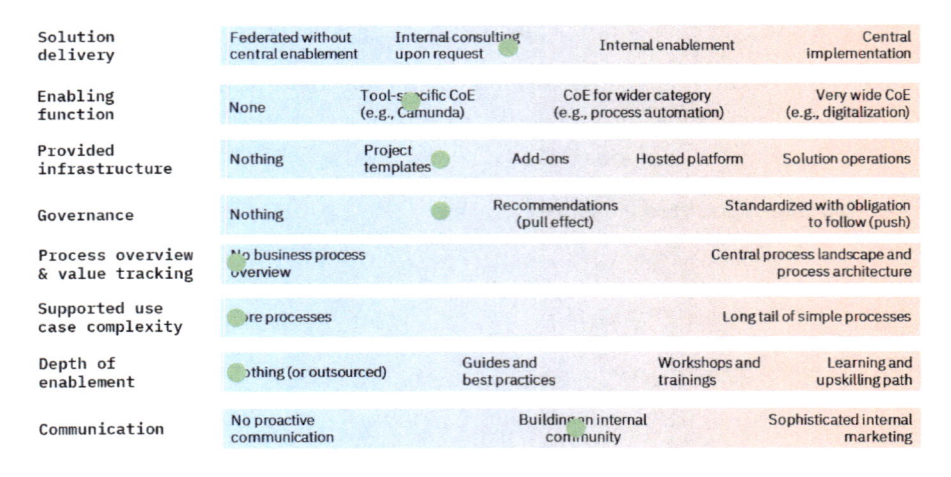

Figure 42: The operating model of an organization that is just forming its CoE

Now it's time to scale the adoption across your enterprise and evolve your CoE accordingly. Typically, at this stage we see more centralization of governance, enablement, and infrastructure and increasingly federated delivery in the business domains. We also see more solutions being implemented in parallel.

The activities of the CoE now include:

- Supporting delivery teams through consulting or providing proactive guidance as a sparring partner (depending on the maturity of the internal customers), but doing less implementation work

- Establishing a helpful governance and reference architecture around process automation applications that teams are happy to use

- Setting up internal workshops and training to bring new users up to speed

- Advising teams on process refactoring and starting to track the business impact of the initiatives

- Growing the community and leveraging it as a feedback instrument for the CoE

- Opening the scope toward wider automation tools or joining forces with other existing CoEs to better serve the evolving needs of the organization

You can see this plotted in Figure 43.

Dimension				
Solution delivery	Federated without central enablement	Internal consulting upon request	● Internal enablement	Central implementation
Enabling function	None	Tool-specific CoE (e.g., Camunda)	CoE for wide category (e.g., process automation)	Very wide CoE (e.g., digitalization)
Provided infrastructure	Nothing	Project templates	Add-ons	Hosted platform	Solution operations
Governance	Nothing		Recommendations (pull effect) ●	Standardized with obligation to follow (push)
Process overview & value tracking	No business process overview		●	Central process landscape and process architecture
Supported use case complexity	Core processes	●		Long tail of simple processes
Depth of enablement	Nothing (or outsourced)	Guides and best practices	Workshops and trainings ●	Learning and upskilling path
Communication	No proactive communication		Building ● internal community	Sophisticated internal marketing

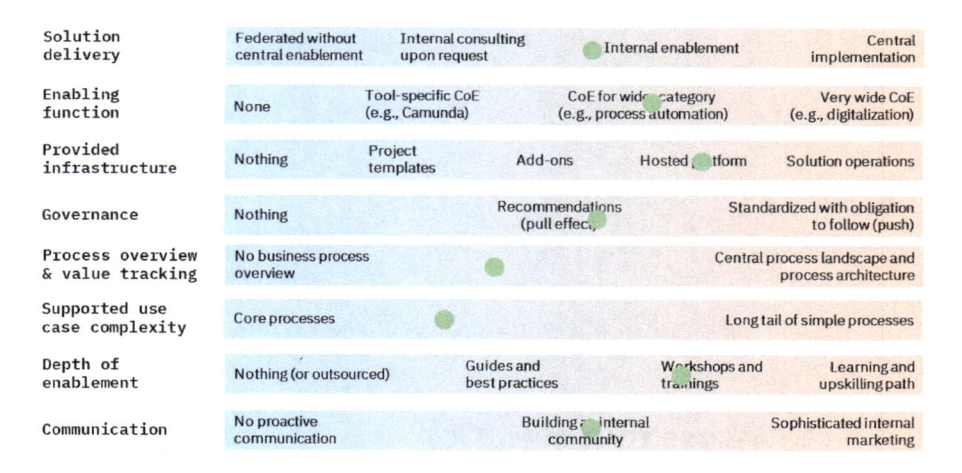

Figure 43: The operating model of an organization with an evolving CoE

The roles are similar to those in a mature CoE, with the size typically ranging between four and eight people:

- CoE lead
- Software developers

105

- IT/solution architects
- DevOps engineers
- Business analysts (BPMN & DMN experts)

The above snapshots are examples that indicate the journey. Exactly where the dots are placed will depend on many factors; the important thing is to move the right dots at the right time in the right direction. The goal is generally to arrive at what we sketched out as our greenfield target operating model at the beginning of this section.

It can be helpful to plot your current state alongside the next or final target state, to help you visualize the steps required to get there. For example, Figure 44 shows the current state (yellow dots) along with the target state (green dots).

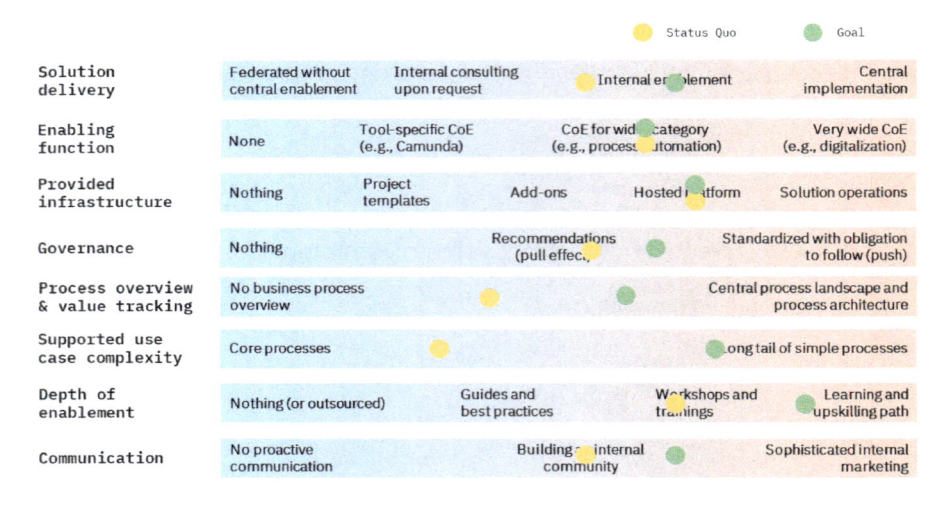

Solution delivery	Federated without central enablement	Internal consulting upon request	Internal enablement	Central implementation
Enabling function	None	Tool-specific CoE (e.g., Camunda)	CoE for wide category (e.g., process automation)	Very wide CoE (e.g., digitalization)
Provided infrastructure	Nothing	Project templates	Add-ons	Hosted platform	Solution operations
Governance	Nothing	Recommendations (pull effect)		Standardized with obligation to follow (push)
Process overview & value tracking	No business process overview			Central process landscape and process architecture
Supported use case complexity	Core processes			Long tail of simple processes
Depth of enablement	Nothing (or outsourced)	Guides and best practices	Workshops and trainings	Learning and upskilling path
Communication	No proactive communication	Building an internal community		Sophisticated internal marketing

Figure 44: Plotting the current and target state together can help you plan your next steps.

Ideally, you will use this as a communication and discovery tool, helping you assess your current level of maturity and keep track of where you are in your process orchestration journey.

Questions to Assess Your Maturity

For people, we describe the five maturity levels as follows (see Figure 3):

- **Level 1:** IT team is not set up to centralize projects or resources.
- **Level 2:** Disparate process orchestration projects are implemented in a decentralized manner (the"sprouting mushrooms" approach).
- **Level 3:** Team seeks to empower business roles to understand their process orchestration projects.

- **Level 4:** A CoE or distributed team focused on repeatability, enablement, and scale has been established.
- **Level 5:** A global CoE acts as a SaaS platform within the organization, providing enablement, training, and internal consulting and developing connectors for process orchestration technology solutions.

Questions you should ask yourself to assess your maturity include:

- TODO

Part III: Technology

Even if we keep stressing that process orchestration, and in fact any kind of organizational transformation, requires more than just technology, technology still plays a vital part in such an initiative. So, this chapter provides a detailed look at the technology you need to successfully leverage process orchestration.

We'll start by exploring enterprise architecture and showing how process orchestration can be the glitter glue for business capabilities to form end-to-end processes. We'll also take a quick look at modern architectural styles, like microservices, and see how domain-driven design (DDD) influences all of this.

Next, we'll examine the tool stack you need to achieve end-to-end process orchestration—most prominently, the process orchestration platform. We will discuss the technical capabilities it brings and what additional capabilities you will need around it. As the whole automation software market is quite dynamic and includes many subcategories, we'll also provide an overview of adjacent tool categories such as robotic process automation (RPA) and explain how they relate to process orchestration.

The primary goal of this chapter is to equip you with the knowledge to sketch out your own architecture and tool stack.

Process Orchestration in Your Enterprise Architecture

Enterprise architecture as a discipline "aligns an organization's structure, processes, information systems, and technology with its strategic objectives and goals" (ChatGPT). To be more concrete, enterprise architecture provides a landscape of business and technical capabilities to solve business problems. You can then create end-to-end processes out of those business capabilities to form value streams that align with your customer journeys.

This is a powerful idea, for various reasons. First, concentrating on end-to-end customer journeys ensures that you don't get lost in internal details that don't matter to your customers. Second, this approach allows for modularity and flexibility, so you can easily adjust how your processes work, add new requirements, and automate and improve them step by step. Third, it allows you to introduce completely new business models or customer journeys as needed.

A business capability in this sense is an *ability to do something*. The important aspect here is that the capability describes the *job to be done*[71], meaning the required business outcome, *not* its implementation. So for example, the billing capability is essential for a company to collect money, but it can be implemented in various ways, such as via an off-the-shelf ERP system or a bespoke microservice. The power of thinking in terms of capabilities is exactly this abstraction from the implementation details. This has significant implications for how you think about end-to-end processes. Let's dive right into this.

Enterprise Architecture: A High-Level View

Figure 45 shows a high-level view of the kind of enterprise architecture we commonly see at our customers.

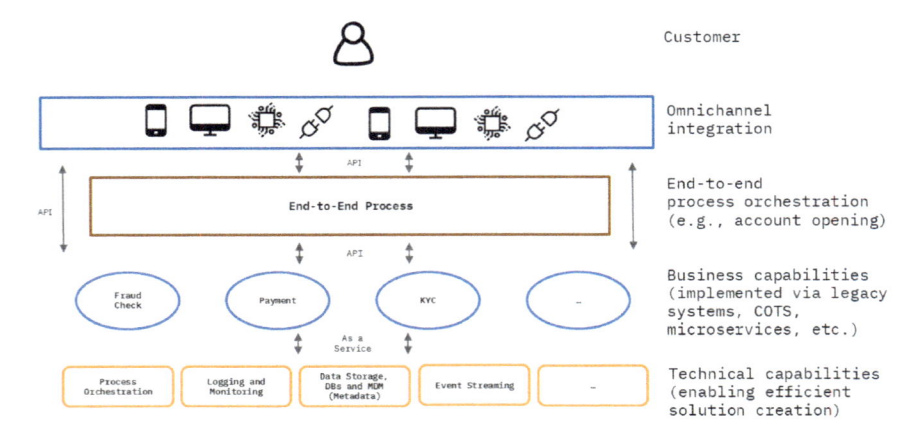

Figure 45: High-level enterprise architecture diagram

Let's roll this up, starting at the bottom.

Technical capabilities

These capabilities enable building applications or services. They include tools such as databases, middleware (e.g., Apache Kafka, messaging, API gateways, etc.), platforms (e.g., Camunda), frameworks, and so on. The cloud services that hyperscalers offer are also in this bucket (e.g., the technical capability to store documents, as implemented in AWS S3 or Azure Blob Storage). The description of the technical capability is abstracted from how it is implemented (or provided) and just indicates what ability needs to be available.

Business capabilities

Business capabilities refer to business functions within your domain. For example, opening a new savings account, granting a loan, and billing are business capabilities. Business capabilities might come in different granularities. For instance, address checking is not a top-level business capability offered to customers (unless your business model is about address checks), but it will be used in many other processes. Business capabilities describe **what can be done** in business terms.

A business capability can be implemented in different ways, as shown in Figure 46. One option is to purchase a commercial off-the-shelf (COTS) solution, to be used either on premises or as a SaaS service in the cloud. For easy integration, the capability should offer an API, typically using HTTP/REST or messaging protocols, depending on the standards defined in your organization (for some legacy systems, RPA is used to make the system invokable). Alternatively, you can develop your own microservices solution or engineer your own software application. You can also leverage low-code tools to implement simple capabilities.

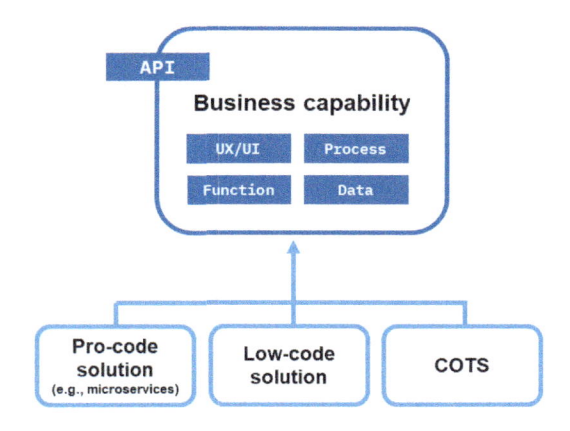

Figure 46: Different options for implementing business capabilities

End-to-end processes

The rubber hits the road in the end-to-end processes of an organization. Those processes should be customer-centric and well aligned with the **customer journey** and corresponding value creation. They need to orchestrate all the activities required to deliver a particular product or service to the customer. For example, ordering a new fixed-line internet service starts with the customer's desire to have internet access, and that desire is only fulfilled once all the necessary hardware is installed and configured and the internet is working for the customer. These processes are also often referred to as **value chains** or **value streams**; only if they are executed properly and in full is real value unlocked. Whenever instances get stuck, there is frustration ("Why is my internet still not working?!") and additional operational costs are incurred (e.g., to support and comfort the customer). This can sometimes also lead to regulatory consequences (e.g., fines when lines are not provisioned according to regulators' SLAs) or even customer churn.

As shown in Figure 45, process orchestration stitches together end-to-end processes out of business capabilities—it's often compared to building a structure out of individual LEGO bricks. This allows you not only to **reuse functionality**, but also to **compose new value chains out of existing capabilities**. It also allows you to **exchange the implementation of a capability** more easily, for example when you want to switch your homegrown subscription billing service for an off-the-shelf SaaS offering. In this example, the end-to-end process can remain the same; only the implementation of the business capability changes.

In a real-life customer scenario at Norddeutsche Landesbank, the enterprise architecture looks like Figure 47.

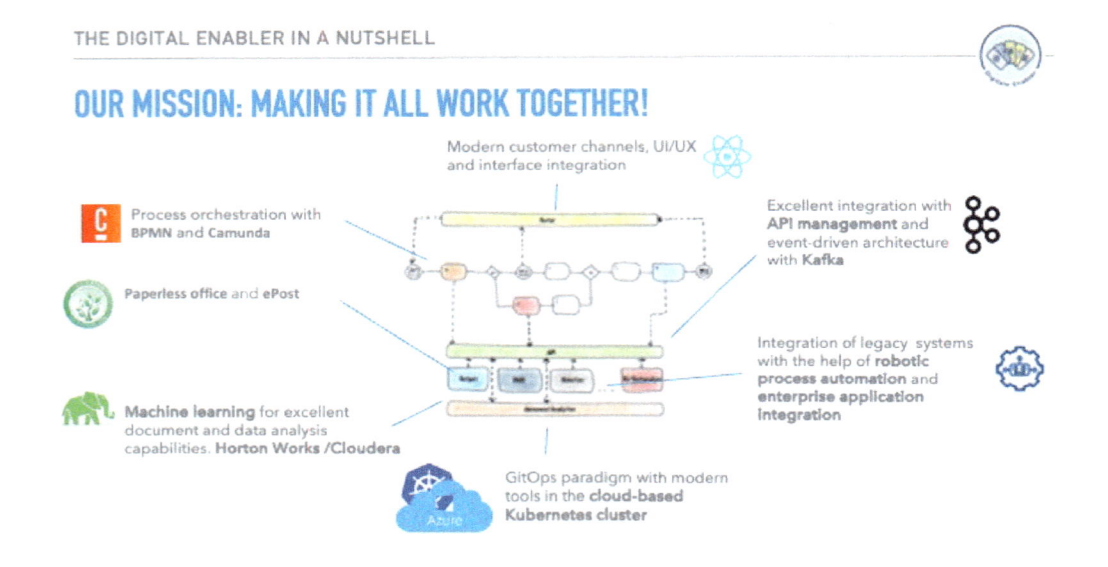

Figure 47: Example customer architecture

Enterprise vs. Solution Scope

Of course, real life is a bit more complicated than the simple architecture diagrams shown above (although that shouldn't stop you from drawing a simplified version like ours if it's helpful to communicate the vision to your internal stakeholders). You'll need to think consciously about the scope of your capabilities.

Typically, **technical capabilities are used by multiple development teams** in the organization, as the technology is mostly domain-agnostic. The same process orchestration platform can very well be used for order fulfillment, billing, and payments, for example. Beside process orchestration, typical examples are databases, document stores, and container orchestrators (like OpenShift). Those technical capabilities are owned by IT and provided as a service to the organization, supported by central CoEs or platform teams. In other words, they have enterprise scope.

Of course, there are exceptions to every rule, so there may be some technical capabilities that are very specifically tied to one domain and as such will only be implemented in a local solution scope. A good example is specific large language models (LLMs) used in the context of AI, e.g. for fraud detection. In this case, the technical capability might directly implement a business capability and not be reused anywhere else (even if your organization has a central enabling team focused on LLMs and AI).

Business capabilities, in contrast, are implemented **for the business domains**, and they should be **owned by the business departments** (solution scope). Commonly, there is still a group in IT that owns the application or microservice that implements a business capability. While this is fine, there should be a clear owner on the business side collaborating closely with IT, as IT cannot manage requirements for those capabilities on its own (in contrast to technical capabilities, where this is feasible). Having the right people involved and good collaboration is key for successful digitalization efforts.

Providing a technical capability around process orchestration as a centralized platform will help you in delivering more business capabilities that leverage process orchestration. In Figure 48, we depict the different scopes and owners involved in building business capabilities as process solutions, where delivery teams can leverage the technical capability of process orchestration.

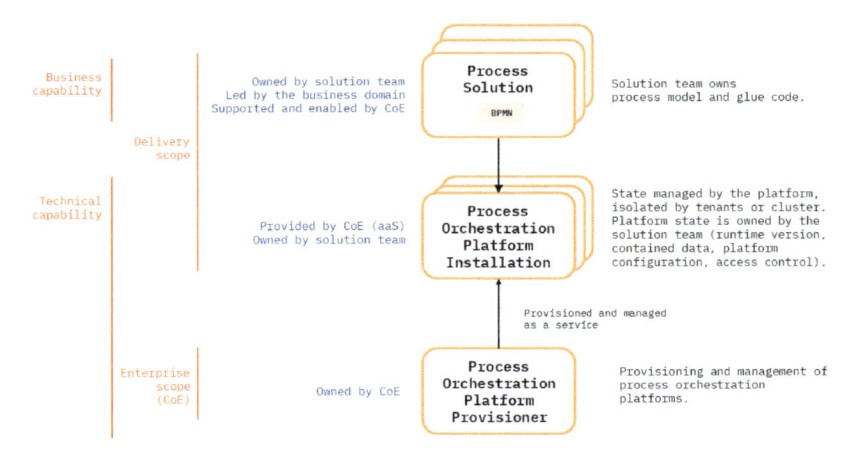

Figure 48: Various scopes and owners of technical and business capabilities

A specific challenge with end-to-end processes is that they always **cross domain boundaries**, making establishing clear ownership hard. One process platform leader at a global bank that had been using process orchestration for several years told us that if they could go back and do anything differently, they would have assigned clear ownership to every process (on a business and technical implementation level) and established a procedure to update that ownership, even in the case of reorganizations.

Process ownership is almost always a little void that needs to be managed properly. Otherwise, you can find yourself in a situation where you have an important capability that nobody owns, meaning nobody can make changes or improvements.

Are Business Processes an Elevated Concept?

A question we regularly see come up is whether business processes should be drawn as elevated concepts above business capabilities in architecture diagrams (like we did in Figure 45), or if a business process is "just another business capability," where the implementation happens to orchestrate other capabilities. It seems that some people have difficulty reconciling these two worldviews.

We recommend that you save your energy by skipping such discussions and taking a pragmatic route. If you want to see end-to-end processes as an elevated concept above the business capabilities, do it; it will work. If you don't like that visualization, don't use it, and just talk about business capabilities. In reality, both approaches are valid—they're just different perspectives on the same reality—and it might be wise to adjust your communication strategy to the audience you are talking to. We can at least agree that sketching a hierarchy of capabilities can be risky in some cases, as the visualization indicates there's a linear relationship, which isn't always the case.

In any event, it is important to note that end-to-end processes are *also* (business) capabilities of an organization, and they might even be tasks in another process. For example, onboarding a new customer might be a standalone process that a customer runs through, but it might also be part of issuing a new insurance policy, and an insurance company might offer very different types of insurance with very different processes implementing those (as visualized in Figure 49).

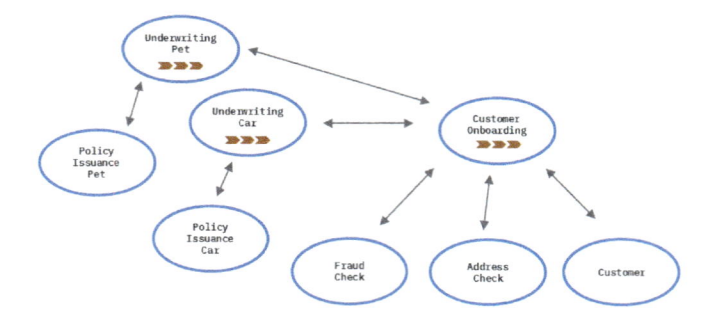

Figure 49: Processes implement business capabilities, and they might also be invoked from other capabilities.

Microservices and Domain-Driven Design

In the last few years there has been a lot of hype around microservices and DDD. Microservices is an architectural style where a complex application is decomposed into smaller, independent services, each focused on a specific business capability. This allows you to scale your development, as you can have many teams, each focusing on one capability only, working as autonomously as possible.

DDD brought a domain focus to the microservices world, advocating to align microservices with domain boundaries. Specifically, DDD defined the so-called bounded context[72]. In a nutshell, with this way of thinking a system is divided into smaller contexts driven by the domain. Within every bounded context, you harmonize wording (using a ubiquitous language[73]) and domain concepts.

If you're thinking this sounds a lot like the architecture diagrams shown earlier, you're absolutely right. Understood properly, a microservices architecture is a great way to implement the above mentioned business capabilities. A key benefit is that you get cross-functional teams assigned to one business capability, making the ownership very clear.

But within the microservices community, there is a similar debate to the one we just discussed: should process orchestration be an elevated concept or not? In this case, the answer to that question has real-world implications: it will influence how you implement communication between the microservices.

We often use an e-commerce example to illustrate this point. Suppose you have an order fulfillment and a payment collection capability. You will create two microservices, each owned by its own development team (Figure 50).

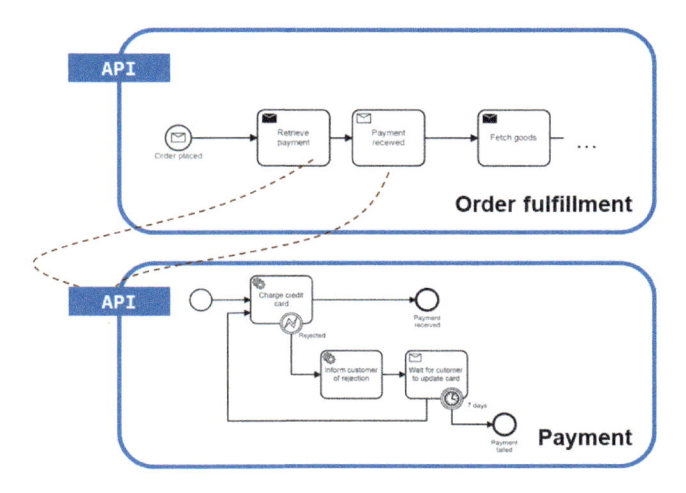

Figure 50: A process within one microservice can orchestrate other microservices via an API, not knowing there are processes inside it.

Looking at the end-to-end business process of order fulfillment, it starts with the original customer's needs and ends with some meaningful end result for them (receiving their order). To get there, the process stretches across the boundary of a single bounded context and involves multiple microservices—in our case, order fulfillment needs to invoke payment collection. This is an interesting problem to look at, and there are two valid viewpoints:

1. The microservice (and the business capability it implements) is the core focus, and it is an implementation detail that process orchestration is used. In this case, order fulfillment and payment are distinct microservices, and order fulfillment simply invokes payment via its API. This gives you complete isolation and team autonomy around implementation choices. You could say that you have two business capabilities, and one (order fulfillment) requires the other (payment) to work. There is still process orchestration at work here, but as an implementation detail within the order fulfillment microservice.

2. The process is an elevated concept, and visibility into the end-to-end process is an important goal. In this case, it might be interesting to invoke the payment process via the orchestration engine directly from the order fulfillment process (a call activity in BPMN). This still allows the different processes to be owned by different teams, but the orchestration engine is now seen as middleware used for communication. This has the upside that visibility around the end-to-end process is improved along the whole toolchain. This has to be weighed against the downside of elevating process orchestration technology to the middleware layer, which basically means removing the option to choose other implementation technologies for individual teams.

Figure 51 illustrates the two viewpoints. Again, both are valid, so which is more appropriate will depend on your organizational setup and architecture goals. (We'd also recommend checking out Camunda's best practice guide to service integration patterns[74] to understand ways to invoke other microservices via API.)

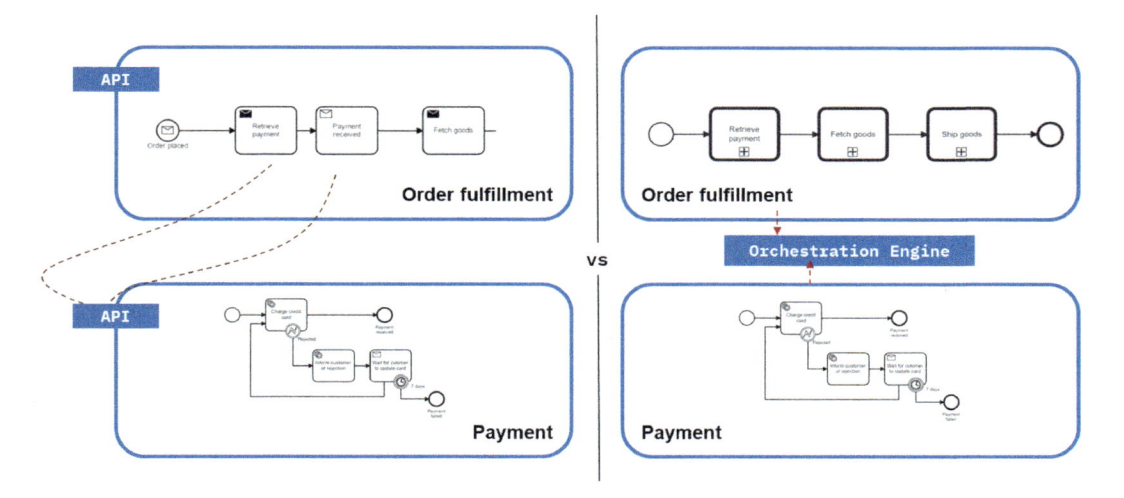

Figure 51: Comparing invoking a subprocess as capability via API, or as subprocess using the orchestration engine

As we mentioned above, the integration via the orchestration engine has some very concrete advantages around **visibility**, as invoking other microservices that have their own processes will be specifically visible in the orchestration tooling. That improves the understanding of the end-to-end process and allows you to drill into subprocesses or investigate the parent process in case of failures.

However, one core thought that is common to both scenarios is that there is **an owning domain (and microservice) for the entire end-to-end process**. This is what makes microservices so interesting from a process orchestration perspective: finally we have an organizational form that defines clear ownership of an end-to-end process, even if it spans multiple organizational silos. This is something that we've seen organizations struggle with for decades. Unfortunately, microservices ownership is mostly confined to the IT side of things—we rarely see business stakeholders being part of the cross-functional team around a microservice, let alone a business person owning the microservice—but still, having a clear process owner is a major benefit.

Agile Approaches Need Architecture Too

Through highlighting the enterprise architecture around process orchestration on the previous pages, we want to address one aspect specifically: the idea that agile approaches work so agilely that they don't need upfront architecture. This belief overlooks the crucial role that upfront architecture plays in ensuring project success, especially within agile frameworks. This is comparable to the role of process design, which is why we bring it up here.

If you want to develop in small iterations, you have to be clear on the goal; otherwise you can easily lose sight of your objective, especially if you go deep into the weeds of implementation.

Take process models as an example. In a first iteration, you might automate just a small portion of the process, or even perform all the steps manually—but you need an idea of what the full process is to even decide on a useful first iteration. It's similar with architecture, especially as many aspects need to be properly defined for even the first iteration (for example, around security, data protection, authentication and authorization, and so on). You need to have an idea of what the risks and potential showstoppers in your architecture are.

In early proofs of concept, we often validate a lot of technical issues that could become showstoppers. Only a good architecture will ensure that a solution can be developed and continuously improved over time. Having an effective enterprise work stream in the form of a CoE can be a big help here, as it might even provide proven solution architectures.

Zooming in on the Process Orchestration Capability

Let's zoom in on the technical capability of process orchestration a bit more to understand the technical components required. As a reminder, Figure 52 shows you at what part of the overall architecture we are looking at.

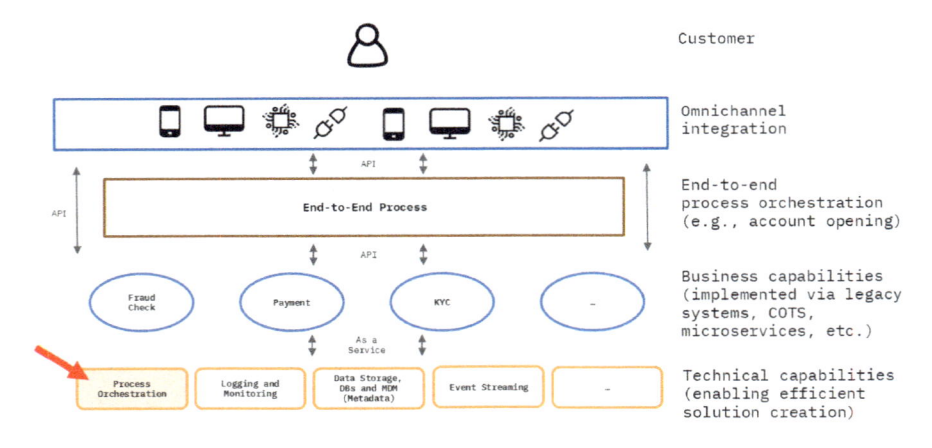

Figure 52: Zooming in on the process orchestration capability

Components Required for Process Orchestration

Figure 53 shows an overview of the different components you may need to support for your process orchestration platform. It groups them into six categories: core process orchestration capability, accelerators, integrations, analytics, InfoSec, and DevOps.

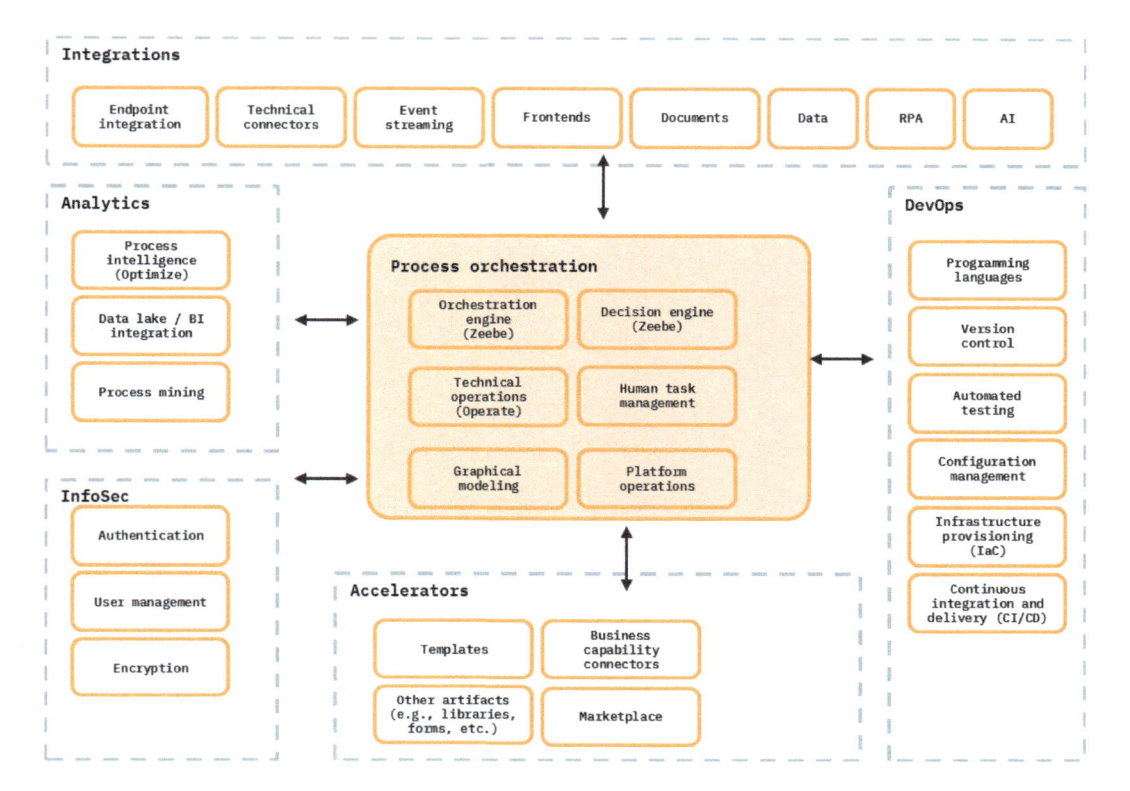

Figure 53: Components required for process orchestration

You'll rarely need to fill in all of these categories, and typically you'll define a roadmap to fill in certain aspects iteratively. For example, business intelligence integration can come at a later stage, and encryption might not be important in your first processes if they don't include sensitive data.

The core process orchestration capability

The process orchestration capability is supported by several concrete components. We'll use the platform we know best (Camunda) as an example, but similar tools should provide comparable components:

- **Process orchestration engine (aka workflow engine):** This is the heart of the platform. It is responsible for defining, managing, and executing the sequence of tasks or steps that constitute the automated process. It ensures that tasks are executed in the correct order and handles dependencies between different steps.

- **Decision engine:** Most orchestration platforms can also execute decision logic in the form of decision tables in DMN, which allows decisions to be automated based on predefined rules and conditions. This is especially useful for scenarios where the automation needs to adapt to changing circumstances or business people want to understand why certain decisions are being made.

- **Human task management:** As processes need to be able to involve people, they also need a way to manage human tasks. In Camunda, this comes in two layers. First, the task management is headless API-based functionality, so that you can query and filter all currently open tasks to show them in your own UI, for example. You can also react to events to push tasks to other systems where they are managed. Second, Camunda provides a Tasklist application[75] and forms[76], which can be used to involve people in processes. The forms can also be embedded in custom UIs using form-js[77]. If you need to build more complex UIs, you will need to connect additional UI technology.

- **Technical operations:** The platform provides tooling to discover, analyze, and solve problems related to process execution. In the case of Camunda, that's Operate[78]. Imagine there is a problem with the service call to the CRM system. You first need monitoring that will recognize that problem, e.g., because incidents are piling up. You will also want to send alerts or integrate with your existing application performance monitoring (APM) tool, so the right person gets notified quickly. In addition to alerting, the tool should support root cause analysis to help you understand the problem at hand (e.g., if some endpoint URL has changed) and fix the issue (e.g., by updating a configuration option and triggering a retry)—and it should be able to operate at scale, because there may be a large number of affected process instances. Developers can also use these tools to play around during development.

- **Platform provisioning:** Platforms need to provide easy ways to be provisioned and operated. Nowadays, this typically means leveraging Kubernetes. In the case of Camunda, for example, it not only provides Helm charts but also a Kubernetes Operator to make the most of the environment.

- **Graphical modeling:** Good BPMN modeling tools are essential to initially design process or decision models, and to add all the necessary details to make them executable. They're typically ubiquitous in the organization and used by a wide variety of stakeholders, from business people to software developers. Good graphical modeling tools also provide collaboration features for discussing or sharing models. Ideally, those tools are provided as web applications so they're easily accessible to a large range of people. Camunda offers both a desktop modeler and a web-based modeler[79] to provide maximum flexibility, as (for example) developers might prefer a tool that works on local files.

Accelerators

In addition to the core platform, accelerators are important to make projects faster. Some of these are provided out of the box by the platform vendor or its community, but accelerators can also be organization-specific, built for example by the CoE. Typical types of accelerators include:

- **Templates:** There are many possible valuable templates. First and foremost, you might find project templates that ease the task of setting up a solution (e.g., a Maven Archetype or a template project to be copied that will be the basis for Java-based solutions). Experience shows that this simple technique can help both to avoid blank paper syndrome with projects and to ensure that company standards are met. As part of this effort, you might also have supporting frameworks or libraries that help with harmonization or standardization (e.g., build tools, Maven parent POMs, Maven BOMs, etc.). Other useful templates might include installation scripts, sample frontends, and even example projects or reference architectures for typical problems. The templates are commonly provided by the CoE and customized to your organization, or you can use templates from your vendor as a basis.

- **Connectors:** Connectors are a great way to accelerate projects, as they bundle glue code for integration in a reusable way. Technical protocol connectors (e.g., for REST or Apache Kafka) allow you to productively implement connectivity, but more powerful are business connectors that have a high level of abstraction in the form of business capabilities. For example, you might have a "Fraud Check Connector" that lets your business people configure relevant inputs in the process model, hiding all the technical details (e.g., that technically it's a REST call underneath).

Increasing the level of abstraction for a connector allows more roles to use that connector in process models. This also enables some level of low code for some processes, which in turn increases flexibility, as such processes can be more easily understood and changed. You can think of it as separating the coded parts (the connector) from the domain logic (the process). The connectors might be provided by the CoE, and federated solution projects can simply use them as needed.

The abstraction of connectors can also form a hierarchy, as the example in Figure 54 shows. The REST connector is a basic protocol connector. Alongside this is a generic Twilio connector that uses REST underneath. Finally, there's a connector to send a text (aka SMS), reduced to only the configuration fields important to business stakeholders; in the background, this connector uses Twilio, which technically means it uses REST.

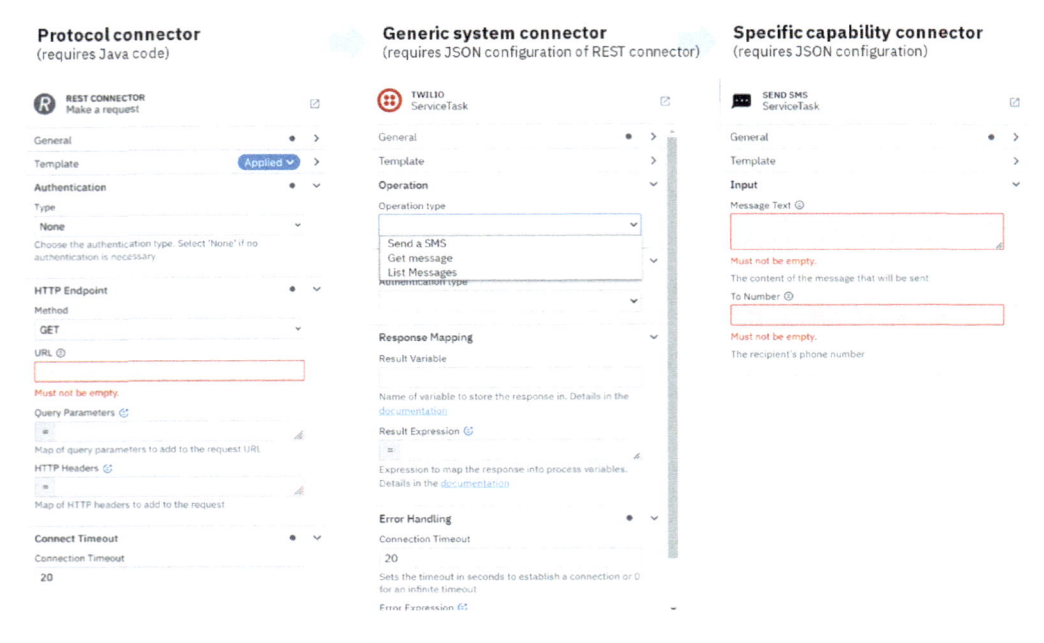

Figure 54: Connectors with different levels of abstraction

- **Marketplace or registry:** If you have templates and connectors, you have to make sure other people can find them. A tool that provides a searchable inventory is very helpful here: as experience shows, a normal wiki can quickly get overwhelmed with the amount of content. In the case of Camunda, for example, there is a marketplace component[80] that is directly integrated with the modeler, so that you can easily search for and use connectors. This can also be operated privately for your organization.

- **Other artifacts:** Organizations can provide further accelerators for all of the other platform components we mention in this chapter, ranging from process endpoints (e.g., user task list integrations or glue code for software endpoints) to DevOps tools (e.g., templates for CI/CD pipelines) or InfoSec integrations (e.g., SSO/LDAP connections). Considering the needs of your delivery teams and providing the right tools through your CoE can get you a long way in improving time to value. You can also leverage best practices like inner-sourcing[81] to share and reuse artifacts created by delivery teams and make them accessible to others.

Integrations

Some capabilities that are interwoven with process orchestration are normally provided by other tools. A good example is that many processes need to store and manipulate data or documents stored in databases or document stores. Common adjacent tool categories include:

- **Endpoint integration APIs and connectors:** The automation solution itself needs to provide an API, but it must also integrate with other systems via their APIs, which we typically call endpoints. Connectors can be provided for this, but it's crucial that the platform is flexible enough to integrate other technologies too, for example by using normal programming code, e.g. in Java.

- **Event buses or streaming platforms:** Many big organizations use event streaming technology within their enterprise architecture (e.g., Apache Kafka or AWS Kinesis). It's vital to connect those platforms with process orchestration, because events from a stream might influence processes, and certain steps in a process might lead to new events being emitted. Technically, this is often easy to do, and out-of-the-box connectors might already do the trick. Otherwise, some glue code can be developed. The goal is that you can easily react to events in your processes and emit new events from your processes (Figure 55).

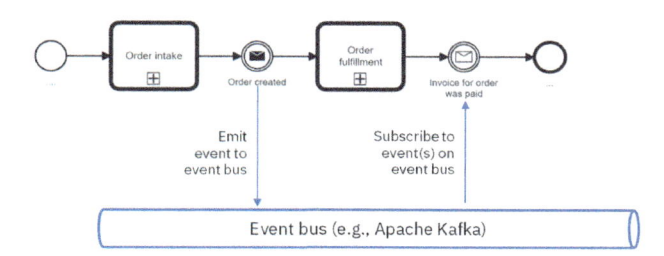

Figure 55: Connecting your process orchestration platform with your event bus

- **Frontends and end user interfaces:** The user interface that can be used by external users (customers) or internal users (e.g., clerks) is the frontend of the automation solution, providing a way for users to interact with and control the automation process. There is often a big difference between customer-facing UIs and internal ones. Sometimes the UI is a command-line interface (CLI). Tasklist applications (also known as todo lists), as mentioned above, can also be part of a custom frontend. Generally speaking, there's a lot of flexibility here: you can use your organization's existing task management software, so that your clerks can keep working with the interface they already use now, or you can create new, custom frontends in any UI technology, either by leveraging typical UI development frameworks (like React.js, Angular, or Vue.js) or by using a low-code UI builder.

- **Data:** Depending on the nature of the automation, a database or other data storage component may be required to store and retrieve information during the execution of the automated process. The process orchestrator persists only minimal data along with process instances, like references or control data that is required to decide about the orchestration flow (see Camunda's best practice guide to handling data in processes[82] for more on this topic). Real domain data needs to be stored outside of the orchestration engine. For that, a database is typically run next to the orchestration engine.

- **Documents:** Many processes interact with documents. The documents may be the driving force (e.g., customer application forms), or they may be summarizing the results (e.g., a case folder), or a mix of both. Documents, like data, should be stored in appropriate systems (e.g., a document management system, AWS S3, SharePoint, etc.) and referenced from the process. Still, they often need to be shown on the frontend to people working with the process.

- **RPA:** Robotic process automation is often mixed up with process orchestration. But as we touched on earlier in this book, RPA is about task automation; that is, automating the execution of a single task in an application that does not provide a proper API. As such, RPA can be very well combined with process orchestration, as the orchestrator will then coordinate the overall process and delegate to RPA for specific tasks. This design also allows you to evolve solutions from manual work to RPA-based automation to true API-led integration—a journey nicely described by Deutsche Telekom[83] at CamundaCon Live 2020 (Figure 56).

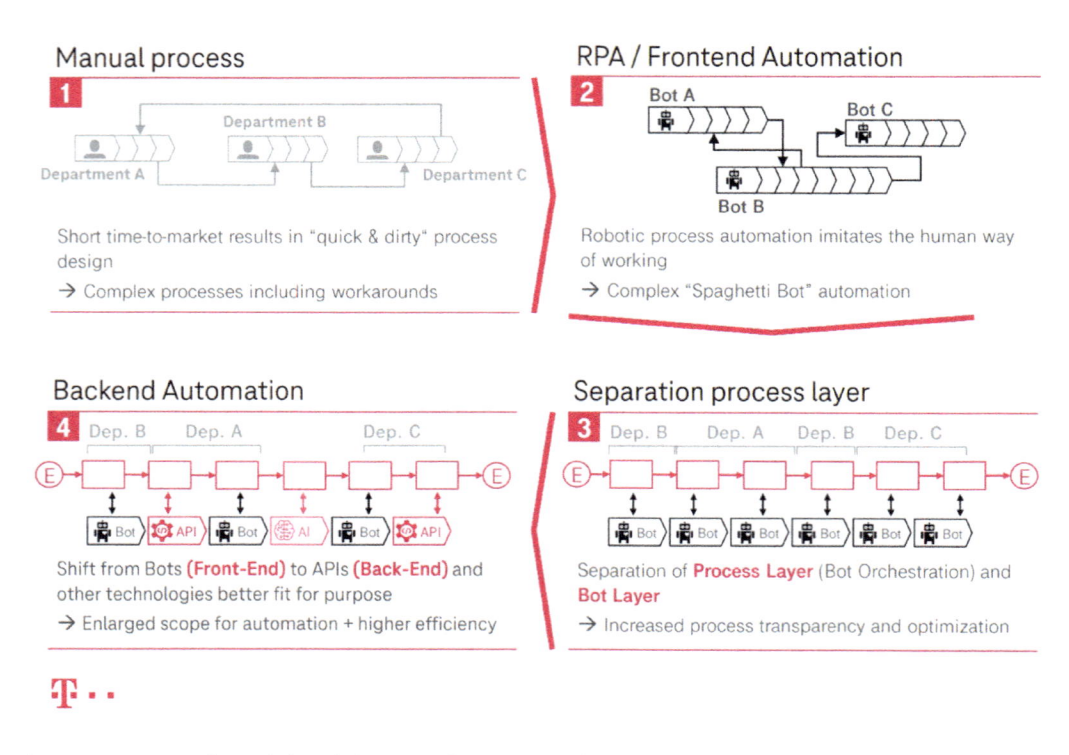

Figure 56: Deutsche Telekom's journey from manual process to RPA to orchestrated bots to true API-based automation

- **AI:** Artificial intelligence, and especially generative AI, will have a huge impact on processes of all sorts over the next few years. As we mentioned in "Enabling Artificial Intelligence" starting on page 29, we believe that for many use cases AI can best be introduced through orchestration. The clarity around the process flow makes it easy to add new AI-based tasks and replace existing ones with AI, perhaps using A/B testing. Technically, the use of AI as an endpoint in a process just requires an API call to the AI platform.

Analytics

Having access to process data is essential for process orchestration because it enables performance monitoring and continuous improvement and provides your business with a real-time view of how your processes are performing. Useful tools in this category include:

- **Process intelligence solutions:** As well as monitoring technical operations and fixing problems that occur at runtime, business stakeholders also need to monitor and improve processes. These personas are typically interested in the overall process performance and its business impact. They might also want notifications around performance indicators like cycle times or waiting time; for example, they need to be notified if a process instance is taking too long and thus will miss its SLA.

  To optimize the overall process, analytics capabilities can provide a clear view of which process paths are used most often, which paths are slow, which data conditions often lead to cancellations, and so forth. This information can be derived from the audit data that a workflow engine stores when executing process instances.

  Process intelligence tooling (e.g., Camunda Optimize[84]) has a clear business process focus and allows the use of graphical process models for everything from analysis to communication.

- **Business intelligence tools:** Most organizations also have generic business intelligence capabilities in use, often centered around data warehouse (DWH), BI, or data lake tooling. The difference from process intelligence is the focus on looking at all data, including object data and events. It is of course also interesting to push audit data from the process orchestration platform to those tools, so it can be put into the context of all the other data; e.g., if you want to cross-reference your process data with financial data to calculate the cost per process instance. If you are interested in how this can be achieved in the context of Camunda, please refer to the best practice guide to reporting about processes[85].

- **Process mining tools:** Process mining is a data-driven methodology that involves the analysis of event logs from information systems to gain insights into executing business processes that were not explicitly visible before. By visualizing the actual paths, deviations, and bottlenecks within processes, process mining can help you identify inefficiencies or problems as well as areas where there is automation potential.

In theory, process mining could serve as a great starting point for process orchestration initiatives. In practice, we don't see that happening often, perhaps because process mining typically looks at log files from core systems like ERP systems to get an overview of how the process is working, but is not wired with applications at runtime. Process mining is also applied by different groups in an organization and rarely connected to automation initiatives. Process tracking, as described in "De-Risking Your Start with Process Tracking" starting on page 52, might be a better approach to use as a basis for automating processes.

InfoSec

TODO: Expand

Look for certification from your vendor (e.g. ISO 27001, SOC 2, and TISAX level 2 certificates).

Furthermore, a clever data design can avoid putting sensitive data into the process orchestration platform in the first place. Often referred to as "privacy by design," this is described in Camunda's best practice guide to handling data in processes[86].

Authentication …

User management …

Encryption …

DevOps

As most process orchestration solutions are software projects too, you also need to take DevOps practices into account. Good process orchestration tools allow you to keep using the best practices you want to use anyway, thereby keeping developers in their comfort zone and ensuring they don't have to learn (many) new skills. The developer comfort zone specifically means:

- **Programming language and environment:** For any reasonably complex automations, you will need to write some code or scripts. The platform should allow your developers to code in the language they are familiar with. This is one of Camunda's superpowers, as it can easily be integrated into different programming stacks (Java, Spring, .NET, NodeJS, etc.).

- **Automated testing:** If the processes you automate are critical, you need automated tests. This is especially important for complex or regulated processes. Test cases will execute a defined set of scenarios and check if their results are as expected. Along the way, they will mock system calls and input data or human decisions. It's best to automate these test cases, so that you can run them as part of your CI pipeline. This allows you to verify that any changes you make are not breaking existing functionality (this is called regression testing). Overall, this leads to much more stable solutions, which in turn gives your developers the confidence to make changes. If you are interested in more technical detail, you can find more information on tests in Camunda's best practice guide to testing process definitions[87].

- **Configuration management:** Process solutions typically require many configuration parameters. One prime example is the endpoint URLs for systems you integrate, which will be different in test, integration, and production environments. Ideally, your solution only uses parameters that can be set during deployment. This is a well-known concept in software engineering, and the Spring framework, for example, has abstractions to grab properties from various places (property files, configuration servers, environment variables, etc.).

- **Infrastructure provisioning:** Infrastructure as code (IaC)[88] is a common way to manage your various systems, from test to integration to production, via code. The installation process itself is then automated via scripts. This allows you to have clearly defined environments that can easily be reproduced. Changes in the setup of those systems are versioned, so they can be easily understood or rolled back in the event of problems.

- **Continuous integration and deployment:** CI/CD practices and tools enable software development teams to automate the process of integrating code changes made in a shared source code repository (continuous integration) and then automatically deploying those changes to production environments (continuous deployment or continuous delivery). This is typically done by so-called *pipelines* in tools like Jenkins or GitHub.

  CI/CD makes sure software can always be integrated and run. As part of that, it runs test cases with every build to make sure nothing has broken. A CI/CD pipeline can also deploy software, even if the individual making the changes does not know how to or is not allowed to integrate or deploy changes. CI/CD pipelines are essential for process orchestration solutions as well, as you will see when we talk about the process lifecycle in "The Software Development Lifecycle and Model Roundtrips" starting on page 157.

Platform Thinking

The process orchestration components described above can be made accessible to delivery teams in the form of an internal platform. In the realm of modern organizational design, platforms are seen as indispensable to reduce cognitive load for development teams and improve time to value (a concept underscored by the previously mentioned *Team Topologies* book[89]). Platforms are the foundational infrastructure required by high-performing teams that produce business value. By providing a common ground for teams to build upon, they promote standardization, reduce friction, and foster a culture of shared responsibility. In short: a platform can be a game changer for automating more with less.

However, a lot of developers we speak with don't have positive associations with the concept of a platform, because of experience with inflexible and proprietary solutions of the past. We will address this in "Why Does This Work Now If SOA Failed a Decade Ago?" starting on page 130, but before diving in the challenges of the past, we first want to point out what makes a good platform. A good read on this is Evan Bottcher's article "What I Talk About When I Talk About Platforms,"[90] on Martin Fowler's blog. According to Evan:

> *A digital platform is a foundation of self-service APIs, tools, services, knowledge and support which are arranged as a compelling internal product. Autonomous delivery teams can make use of the platform to deliver product features at a higher pace, with reduced coordination.*

Please keep the following key characteristics of a good platform in mind when you create your own internal offering:

- **Self-service:** A good platform can be used in a self-service way by delivery teams. The goal is to avoid what Evan calls *backlog coupling*, where the delivery team needs to raise tickets with the platform that need to be prioritized properly so as not to hinder the delivery team's progress. Seeing the platform as a product, with proper product management, is also very important to make sure the platform serves the most important user needs (the users are the internal delivery teams!), but at the same time is not overengineered.

- **Compelling to use:** A platform should provide great support that delivery teams are happy to use, because it solves a problem for them that would be hard to solve otherwise. Evaluating technology for process orchestration and automation, setting it up, and defining your solution architecture is hard work—most delivery teams are happy to just follow the recommended way of doing things, if that path is properly described. This is an approach we've seen at many companies; Spotify describes them as golden paths[91] and Twilio and Netfix as paved paths[92]. Teams in those organizations do not have to make use of the provided platform, but they're responsible for the costs of maintaining their own alternatives.

- **Flexible:** A platform should not enforce an inflexible way of working. Teams might need to configure the platform in a specific way, or extend it; they should be able to do whatever is necessary so that the platform is an actual help, not an obstacle to use.

- **Easy to get started:** In addition to self-service capabilities, you should provide users with additional help to get started with the platform, like tutorials, guides, examples, or templates. This content also needs to be maintained and evolved, which is typically done by the CoE.

- **Rich community:** The platform should have a rich internal community, backed by an international community around core products used in the platform. This also means that the platform should use out-of-the-box functionality of the core components whenever possible, to make sure users can find help not only via internal resources but also with a simple web search.

- **Secure and compliant:** A core advantage of having your own platform is that you can make sure you meet all important security and compliance requirements. This can be proven to pass regulatory checks.

- **Operated professionally:** For wide acceptance internally, the platform must, of course, work properly.
- **Up-to-date and maintained:** The underlying software components must all be kept up-to-date. It's better to keep the scope of your platform minimal and invest resources in maintenance than to have many features that are half-baked. For example, you should prioritize keeping your Camunda version up-to-date over adding more features around Camunda, as this is typically more mission-critical in the long run.

In his article, Evan describes the responsibilities of the solution (or application) teams and the platform team as follows:

> *Application teams build, deploy, monitor, and are on call for the application components and application infrastructure that they provision and deploy on the platform. Platform teams build, deploy, monitor, and are on call for the platform components and underlying platform infrastructure.*
>
> *The platform team ideally doesn't even know what applications are running on the platform, they are only responsible for the availability of the platform services themselves.*

Another good take on this is the article "Run Your Platform Like a Business Within a Business"[93] by Rosalind Radcliffe et al.; it highlights the significance of treating internal platforms as products and developers as customers, emphasizing principles such as development, marketing, sales, delivery, and support to ensure successful adoption and utilization within organizations.

One final important thought we want to call out with regard to building your platform is raised in the article "What Is Platform as a Product?"[94] from the authors of the *Team Topologies* book[95]: when building the platform you should collaborate closely with solution projects in the beginning, but switch to a product-as-a-service model as soon as possible (Figure 57).

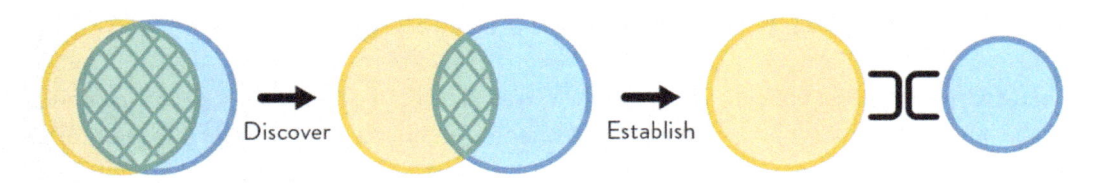

Figure 57: Strong collaboration with solution teams is required for the evolution of the platform, but the platform should then be provided as a service (from "What Is Platform as a Product?")

This is what we also recommend CoEs doing: participate in the early projects until you've learned enough to part ways, then have a central CoE that enables other projects in the organization.

Modern Process Orchestration Platforms Don't Become a Bottleneck

From real-life projects, we know the concerns around centrally run platforms. Many organizations have had bad experiences with proprietary, monolithic tools in the past. One example is the BPM suites that were popular a decade ago: such tools were operated centrally, but also required very specific knowledge so that only a central team could work with them. This meant those tools frequently turned into a bottleneck on two levels: organizationally, as that one team could not do everything it was asked to do, and technically, as the tool was simply not scalable enough to run the load it was supposed to run.

It is important to understand that we have a totally different situation today, for various reasons:

1. Modern platforms are **scalable** enough to run big workloads.

2. A good multitenant design allows tools to **isolate** teams from each other if they have specific requirements (we'll talk more about this in "Isolation Needs and Multitenancy" starting on page 134).

3. A good tool has **backward-compatible** APIs, meaning that when the platform itself is updated, this does not affect the delivery teams using the platform. So, for example, the platform team can install important security patches without disrupting the delivery teams, and delivery teams do not need to worry about the health of the platform.

4. Platform teams focus on enablement, making the tool as **self-service** as possible. This means the delivery teams are not slowed down but rather accelerated by those teams.

Thanks to these characteristics, a centrally operated process orchestration platform—done right—does not cause any kind of bottleneck.

Why Does This Work Now If SOA Failed a Decade Ago?

Let's address the other typical concern we hear: Wasn't all of this also one of the core promises of the business process management/service-oriented architecture (BPM/SOA) duo many organizations tried and failed to successfully apply 15 years ago? Why should it work now? What has changed?

The big problem back around 2010 was that the whole idea was very vendor-driven and tool-centric. Big vendors sold SOA platforms, enterprise service bus (ESB) products, BPM suites, service registries, and whatnot. Customers were locked into highly proprietary environments that their technologists could not handle (this was touched on, for example, in Bernd's blog post "The 7 Sins of Workflow"[96]). At the same time, IT was driving this change without involving the business or changing the culture respective to the way they built software. This led to a situation where organizations kept working the way they had been, but using a more complex tool stack that their developers could not handle. The rest is history.

We have a very different situation today, thanks to developments in the following areas:

- **Agility:** As well as theoretical knowledge, practical applications of agile practices around iterative development, minimal viable products (MVPs), and continuous improvement are everywhere now. Important groundwork like the previously mentioned book *Accelerate*[97] proves that agile practices are essential for companies to survive.

- **DevOps:** DevOps evolved from a set of practices aimed at improving collaboration between development and operations teams to a cultural and organizational movement, emphasizing automation, continuous integration, and continuous delivery for faster and more reliable software delivery. Books like *The Phoenix Project*[98] by Gene Kim, Kevin Behr, and George Spafford helped many people around the globe to understand its value.

- **Best-of-breed:** The tide is turning against big monolithic products and vendors. While to some extent we are seeing proprietary software components again with the big hyperscalers (AWS, Azure, GCP, etc.), companies in general no longer accept proprietary and monolithic stacks for core functionality like process automation. Instead, they look for the best solutions available for each specific purpose.

- **Products instead of projects:** A mindset shift has begun among internal development teams around providing reusable assets. The idea is that their software should be treated like a product, and in fact, it should be OK to swap internally provided software with off-the-shelf products or SaaS services if possible. Sometimes, those products developed in-house can even be offered externally as services to third parties. This worldview changes how a team manages its software (distribution, documentation, collecting and prioritizing requirements, etc.). Providing products is a key success factor, and it incentivises teams to create products their users love to use. The alternative is maintaining a reusable service and being annoyed by users constantly coming up with questions or ideas for improvement that could mean additional work. Mik Kersten's book *From Project to Product*[99] is a good read on this, describing the paradigm shift in software development from project-based thinking to a product-centric approach. Kersten argues that aligning software delivery with business goals and customer needs, focusing on continuous delivery, and adopting value stream thinking are essential for organizations to thrive in the digital age.

- **Microservices and domain-driven design:** As we described earlier in this chapter, the architectural style that enables dividing big, monolithic systems into smaller, independent services has greatly matured over the last decade, with an increased understanding of how to design boundaries that help, rather than just adding technical challenges.

- **SaaS and cloud:** Leveraging SaaS offerings and moving workloads to the cloud is now happening on a broad scale. While many organizations were still pretty skeptical about this a few years ago, today we're seeing customers in all industries moving to the cloud in a big way. This approach makes it much easier to take advantage of new capabilities, be they business or technical, as there is no installation to be done or operations team required. You can use services almost instantly, if there's a sound business case for it. Most organizations are also increasing their maturity on settling legal questions around SaaS to enable teams to adopt these offerings more easily (without compromising on compliance and IT security).

All of those developments combined now allow a way of working that enables the architectural vision sketched out in this book.

And to be fair, looking back, not all BPM and SOA initiatives really failed. We have seen customers achieve great results with that approach, largely by applying a lot of the same ideas and techniques we just mentioned. For example, we've seen best-of-breed development stacks using developer-friendly tools like Camunda and Apache Camel, mastering a working CI/CD pipeline, and developing great internal guidance around service design, domain boundaries, and discovery, leading to highly successful business outcomes.

Operating and Providing a Process Orchestration Platform

Let's switch gears now and assume you want to run a process orchestration platform in your own organization. This section dives into the practical questions you'll have to answer to do this. While we'll use the Camunda platform as an example to avoid too much theoretical palaver, the main points are also true for other tools.

Running a Platform Like Camunda

Figure 58 shows a typical Camunda deployment. To run Camunda itself, you'll ideally use the Camunda SaaS offering. In this case, you don't have to deal with installation and operation of the platform as a whole.

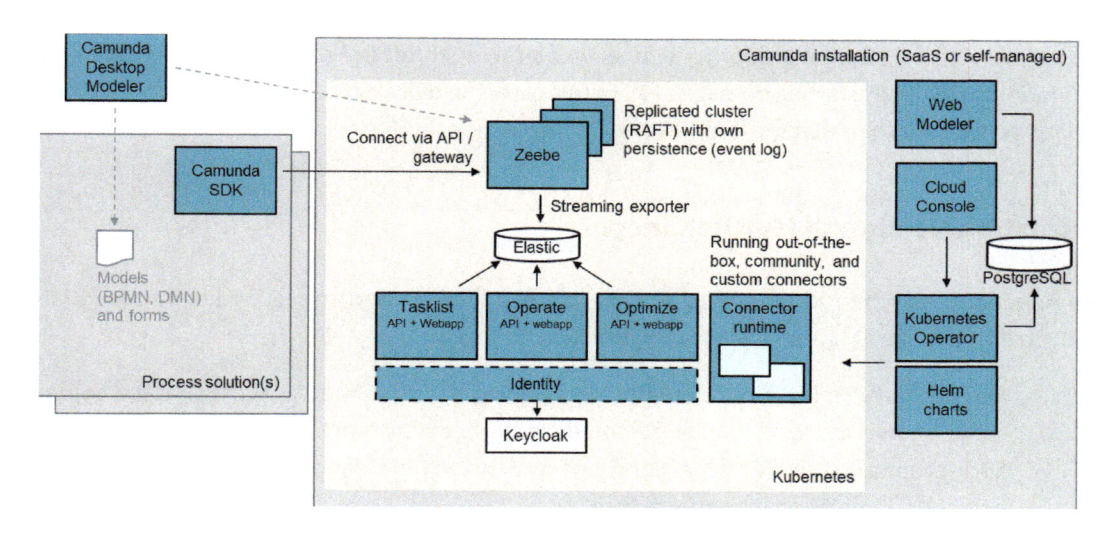

Figure 58: A typical Camunda deployment

Unfortunately, however, some organizations still have reservations about using SaaS, even if the business case is compelling. One common concern is around information security and data residency—but this can be addressed. Camunda, for example, holds ISO 27001, SOC 2, and TISAX level 2 certificates to comfort InfoSec stakeholders. Furthermore, a clever data design can avoid putting sensitive data into the orchestration engine in the first place, as described in Camunda's best practice guide to handling data in processes[100]. This is often referred to as "privacy by design."

Another common situation is that development teams are put off by the perceived effort involved in getting approval for a SaaS platform. Those teams may consider it easier to install everything themselves, as this can be organized within IT, in their comfort zone. While this is understandable, it is typically not a good choice in terms of total cost of ownership (TCO) for the overall organization—and especially if you look at the enterprise scope, where you will end up running many installations, it's shortsighted.

At the same time, when customers start to really push for SaaS usage in their organization, they're usually positively surprised at how easy it is to get approval in the end. And this is a great deal: Putting in a little effort now will save you a lot of internal maintenance effort on your own installation for years to come. So, when you're evaluating the infrastructure for your enterprise initiative, you should definitely give SaaS some consideration, to drive efficiencies and standardization in your operations.

If SaaS is definitely not possible for your situation, you can install Camunda self-managed[101]. This is typically done on Kubernetes (e.g., OpenShift) using the provided Helm charts. While Camunda tries to ease the whole installation procedure, this is not something that should be handled by delivery teams, as it's not directly connected to business benefits. Instead, we recommend that your CoE sets up the platform—and, even better, operates it—for the delivery teams (see "Platform Thinking" starting on page 127). In this case, the delivery teams are effectively using a SaaS service, just one that's offered internally.

Isolation Needs and Multitenancy

Independent of how you set up the process orchestration platform, you need to decide what level of isolation your solutions need (Figure 59):

- **No isolation:** Multiple solutions work on one big cluster. While this is the simplest setup, it also bears risks, for example that solutions might define processes with the same identifiers, that operators might get confused by a mix of different processes, or that a noisy neighbor[102] might affect performance.

- **Logical isolation through multitenancy:** To guarantee at least minimal isolation you can set up tenants, so that every solution uses its own tenant. This means they're on the same physical hardware but are isolated logically. This is advisable as it gives each solution its own namespace and makes operators' lives easier. It also saves on hardware costs compared to running dedicated clusters.

- **Physical isolation through separate clusters:** You can also run a separate installation for every solution. By doing so, you guarantee that only that solution uses the cluster's hardware. This is typically useful for use cases that have high load requirements, are sensitive to latency, or have regulatory requirements around isolation.

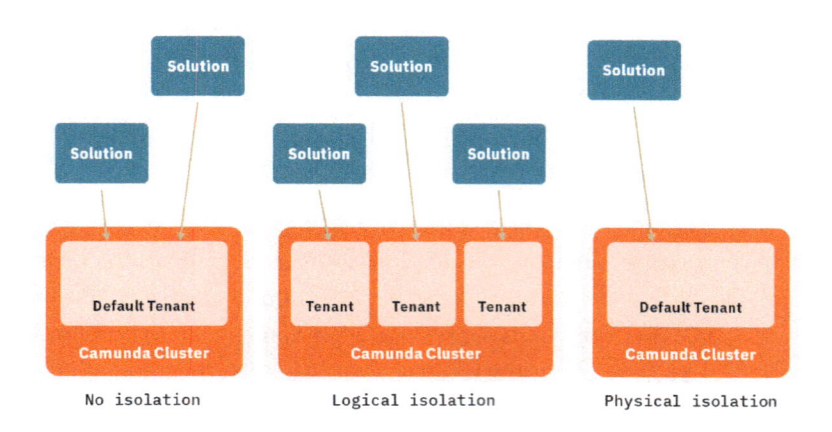

Figure 59: Different levels of solution isolation

Of course, you can mix these styles. Most customers use physically isolated clusters only for selected use cases—typically "dark red" (i.e., complex, mission-critical processes, according to our categorization in "A Useful Categorization of Use Cases" starting on page 33)—and tenants for all other solutions. For development environments, every developer also gets their own tenant to avoid conflicts or side effects when multiple developers work on different aspects within the same process model.

Figure 60 shows a typical example of how customers assign workloads to clusters and tenants in the banking domain. As you can see, departments have separate clusters, which is not necessary but often makes things easier as it requires less coordination. Solutions typically each get their own tenant, even if they are in the same domain. Note that in this setup you cannot use call activities for communication between solutions (as discussed in "Microservices and Domain-Driven Design" starting on page 115).

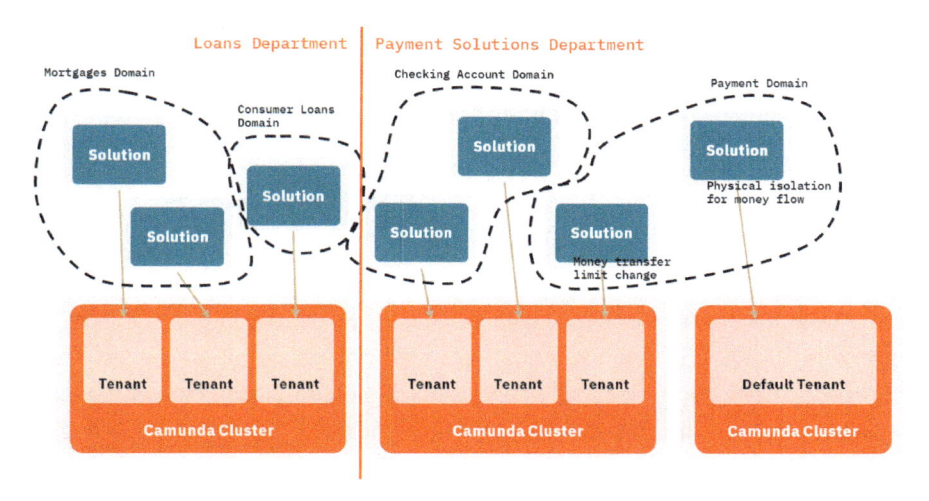

Figure 60: A typical setup of clusters/tenants in the banking domain

Staging Environments

Most customers run three stages for their solutions:

- **Dev:** We strongly recommend using development clusters to avoid development using production systems. While developers can also work with local installations, in most cases it is easier to leverage SaaS environments that offload installation and operation responsibilities from the developer. Developers should have their own personal environments, isolated from what other developers are doing, to avoid errors (e.g., due to versioning conflicts with multiple developers working on one cluster). This can be achieved using separate tenants.

- **Int:** On top of functional unit tests performed by developers, most customers want to run integration tests in a close-to-real-life environment. This should be in its own cluster or tenant. This installation does not necessarily require a lot of hardware and using a tenant typically works fine, as this is normally sufficient to run testing workloads. However, the environment needs to be isolated against other test runs to avoid any side effects. Make sure not to run performance tests in such environments.

- **Prod:** The production environment is typically clustered for high availability and resilience.

Of course, there can be additional environments or stages. The prime example is test environments. Take functional unit tests: they ideally run in a completely self-contained way, without requiring any external components. With Camunda, for example, you can write JUnit tests in Java and use a testing extension[103] that will run the orchestration engine in-memory for the unit tests. This ensures they will always run in a clean environment and will not need any external elements to work. Or customers running performance tests for performance-critical solutions need a specific performance test cluster that is sized and configured like a production cluster. Those tests should then be run independently of functional or integration testing.

Sizing and Scaling

More than anything else, how you size your environment will depend on the actual tool you're using. For example, Camunda is built for scale, but it is also perfectly fine to run small use cases on it. A good rule of thumb is that if you have less than one process instance per second, you don't really need to think about scale but can just run the smallest cluster setup available. If you are interested in more specific details, check out Camunda's best practice guide to sizing your environment[104]. This gives you an idea of what load a cluster can handle, and what hardware you need to provision if you run it self-managed. It also dives into bigger environments and how to do load tests and benchmarks if scale matters to you. To give a rough example (and prove wrong people who still think orchestration engines are slow), we have customers running more than 10,000 process instances per second on one cluster.

Resilience and High Availability

How resilience is achieved also depends heavily on the tool in use. In the case of Camunda, the core architecture of the platform is engineered so that you can scale horizontally and build resilient setups. By default, Camunda clusters run three nodes and can tolerate the absence of one node. Those nodes can easily be distributed geographically to achieve various levels of resilience. Possible configurations are:

- **Single-zone:** You build a cluster of nodes in one zone. You can stand hardware or software failures of individual nodes.
- **Multizone:** You distribute nodes into multiple zones, increasing availability as you can now stand an outage of a full zone (i.e., data center). Zone outages are very rare.

- **Multiregion:** You distribute nodes into multiple regions (i.e., geographically distributed data centers). You will likely never experience an outage of a full region, as this might only happen because of exceptional circumstances.

We typically see multiregion requirements because of legal obligations, not so much because of practical matters. Keep in mind that this setup will survive the loss of all data centers in one region. Typically, in those scenarios the goal is to reduce manual cleanup work after an outage, not to eliminate any manual intervention. To be clear, multiregion setups are not a solution for serving customers in different regions faster, as the engine still needs to synchronize between regions, which cancels out any latency that might be saved upfront.

More information on resilient setups can be found in the blog post "How to Achieve Geo-Redundancy with Zeebe."[105]

Selecting the Right Process Orchestration Technology

There are different types of tools that will generally help you automate processes, but in very different ways, for very different situations. Unfortunately, the lines between different tool categories are blurry, and the category boundaries may differ depending on whom you ask. Let's try to sort this out a little bit.

We'll start by sketching out the typical decisions you need to make when selecting a process automation tool, as visualized in Figure 61. The following subsections dive into the details.

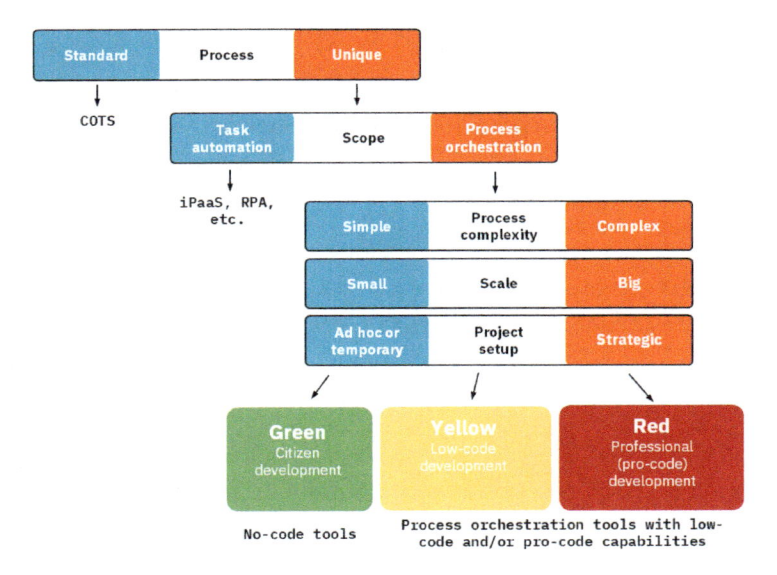

Figure 61: Important decisions around tool selection

Types of Processes: Standard vs. Tailor-Made

One of the first questions to ask yourself is the following: Do you want to automate standard processes, or do you need tailor-made automation?

Every organization has standard processes, for example around payroll, tax statements, and absence management. These processes are more or less the same in every company, which is why you can simply buy standard COTS software to automate them. For instance, at Camunda, we use Spendesk to manage expenses, automating much of the process around expense management (e.g., receipts collection, approval, reimbursement, etc.).

In contrast, your core value-driving processes might be unique to your company and require tailor-made solutions. A great example is NASA and its Mars robot[106]. The processes to handle data from the robot and calculate the robot's movements are pretty unique; very few organizations on the planet do this. In this case, the uniqueness is rooted in the fact that NASA has a very **unique business model**. But of course, more down-to-earth processes can also be highly specific to certain organizations. This is frequently the case if you are a first mover in your industry; for example, the first retail bank to fully automate trade requests.

Besides the business model, processes may be unique because they involve a **unique set of IT systems**, typically because of existing **legacy systems** that are in use. Take, for example, the customer onboarding process in a bank. Even if much of the required functionality is available in core banking systems, a unique set of integration requirements (for example, with your legacy mainframe system) can make the process highly individual and complex. The same is true for claim handling in an insurance company; the process may be very similar but still look quite different from organization to organization, depending on the involved systems and process steps.

If you can automate your end-to-end processes with commercial off-the-shelf software, do this. It's probably the cheapest option. Just keep in mind that this will preclude you differentiating your organization via those processes, as your competition may well be using the same ones.

If your processes are special, however, you need tailor-made process orchestration. As a rule of thumb, tailor-made solutions are more often required for core processes, like in the customer onboarding or NASA cases, than for supporting processes like absence management. The latter are seldom unique enough to justify tailor-made solutions, as deviations rarely make the business more successful (exceptions confirm the rule, of course).

Core processes don't *have* to be unique, though. Imagine a small web shop selling sustainable bike helmets made out of coconut fibers (we just made this up). The product is super innovative, but the core order fulfillment process can be standard; an off-the-shelf Shopify account might be all the company needs.

In sum, the answer to the question of whether to use a standard software or tailor-made process orchestration is: it depends! If you want to differentiate your organization or have custom requirements, go for tailor-made process orchestration; otherwise, you're probably better off adapting your way of working to how a process is automated in standard software.

Scope: Task Automation and Simple Integrations vs. Processes

The next question to ask yourself is: Do you only need to automate tasks or do local integrations, or do you need to orchestrate end-to-end processes?

We alluded to the difference between process orchestration and task automation earlier, in "Process Automation = Process Orchestration + Task Automation" starting on page 20. Plenty of tools can automate specific tasks, and many of them can trigger follow-up tasks as a result of a task's execution. This theoretically allows the automation of complete processes with such tools. But there are serious limitations: the overall process is not visible, and complex processes cannot be addressed because they require complex orchestration logic. Additionally, tools for task automation don't do any kind of state handling to support long-running processes.

There are multiple flavors of task automation and simple integration tools. These include:

- **Application integration tools:** These tools (e.g., Zapier, IFTTT, Tray.io, Integromat) can execute actions when some event happens—for example, inserting new data into Airtable when a Trello card is completed. Some of these tools extend beyond the boundary of task automation, also providing basic process automation capabilities (e.g., Tray).

- **Integration platform as a service (iPaaS) tools:** These are typically cloud-based platforms (e.g., Mulesoft, Boomi) that allow integration on a point-to-point basis. They provide prebuilt connectors, data mapping, and transformation capabilities, but don't consider the end-to-end process.

- **Technical task automation frameworks:** These frameworks (e.g., Apache Camel) ease the job of a developer for certain tasks, like communication with the filesystem, messaging middleware, and other interface technologies. Batch processing also fits into this category, as a (outdated) way to automate tasks with batch jobs that apply them to, say, every row in a certain dataset.

- **RPA tools:** These are so commonly confused with process orchestration tools that they get their own section ("Robotic Process Automation (RPA)" starting on page 142).

All of these types of tools can be used in addition to a process orchestration platform to solve integration challenges, but they should not be considered a replacement.

In short, if you're looking at end-to-end processes, you need to look at process orchestration tools.

Process Complexity: Simple vs. Complex

At this point in the decision tree shown in Figure 61, you've determined that you want to go for tailor-made process automation. To select the right tool category and specific tool, one important factor to look at is process complexity.

Processes vary hugely in complexity. For example, one of this book's authors runs a personal process around speaking at conferences. A list of conferences is maintained in Airtable, and some additional Zaps (integration flows in Zapier) automate important parts of the call-for-papers process; for example, to remind them on Slack when a call for papers is about to expire, or to ask for the final slide deck to publish online. These processes are relatively simple and deal with a very limited set of applications, all of them with well-known cloud connectors. This makes it a great use for low-code tooling.

Compare this to an end-to-end business process, like a tariff change for a telecommunication customer that not only needs to take complex pricing rules into account but also interact with many different bespoke IT systems (e.g., to enter the changes into CRM or billing systems, or to provision changes to the telecommunication infrastructure). Or consider the core money flow or trading processes of a bank: they not only need to orchestrate many different systems but also need to run super reliably at scale, 24/7, while fulfilling regulatory requirements. Those processes definitely require a software engineering approach to process orchestration in order to be able to tame the complexity and deliver the quality you need.

Generally speaking, there are different drivers of complexity:

- The **number and nature of systems, applications, or people** involved in the process. For systems and applications, their own complexity and ease of integration is especially important. There's a big difference between connecting to a well-known cloud tool like Salesforce and a legacy mainframe application that's a black box. For people, the complexity of the user interface needs to be taken into account; some processes might not need any UI and some only simple forms, whereas in other cases you might need a fully fledged single-page application to support the users.

- The **number and complexity of activities** involved in the process, and the **control structures** required (e.g., the number of branching points, errors, or exceptions that need to be handled, or the need for advanced constructs like event handling or compensation).

- The **amount and nature of data** handled in the process. This can range from simple text fields to complex documents.

- The **number of developers** required to work on a project.

- The **number of departments** or people involved in discussing how a process is implemented.

- The **number of users** that do operational work as part of the process instances, e.g. via human tasks.

- **Compliance or regulatory requirements**. For example, financial processes often need to comply with many legal requirements. Auditors might not only ask about how processes are implemented in general, but also want to look at audit logs to understand what has happened in certain situations.

The more complex the processes are, the more best practices from software engineering you will need to handle them. In contrast, simple processes can also be handled by low-code tooling, where you simply put together a process from standard elements.

Scale: Small vs. Big

Scale is the next aspect to consider. Scale can relate to various things. To avoid confusion, we'll limit it to "load" in this context—so, essentially the number of process instances in a certain time frame. Some consider the number of systems or teams involved as part of "scale," but we explicitly put those factors into the discussion of complexity above.

For example, one of our customers implements a process that must be able to handle two million payments per hour[107]. This is definitely a big scale and involves considerably different requirements than the management of the abovementioned handful of calls for papers a month. First and foremost, the chosen technology must be able to handle the targeted scale and help you navigate failure scenarios at scale; for example, if a core system faces an outage and many thousands of process instances need to be retriggered once it comes up again.

Volatile loads might lead to further requirements around elasticity, so you need to keep potential changes to the scale in mind. For example, if you provide some service via the internet and run a successful ad, you want your delivery process to be ready to scale to meet the increased demand without interruptions.

Project Setup: Ad Hoc vs. Strategic

As part of the overall Camunda journey, our marketing teams grew quite a bit over the last few years. We hired more people, introduced new functions, and explored a heck of a lot of new ideas about what to do. Many of those ideas required some IT support. During such an exploratory phase, you have no idea what idea will turn out to make the most sense or exactly what the process will ultimately look like. So, we did a lot of manual work, but also applied low-code tooling in areas that could be automated. We didn't aim for a stable solution that could run for years; we just needed something quick and dirty to explore or validate an idea. We were fine with the fact that only one individual—the original creator—really understood the temporary solution. And we knew it would need to be shut down in a few months, at most.

But when we understood what really worked, we needed to scale that approach. It became strategically important and required a sustainable and maintainable solution. This was the moment when we moved toward properly engineered orchestration.

Another good example of ad hoc processes is one-time-only tasks. Maybe you need to run a data cleansing operation just once, then throw it away. Of course, you have less requirements on the stability and maintainability of this process.

At the other end of the spectrum are the organization's core processes. These are very strategic. Many organizations have entire departments responsible for operating and maintaining single processes. Consider again the example of processing two million payments per hour—that's not something you could ever do on an ad hoc basis.

Part of the decision, then, might also be based on the criticality of the process. If a process is critical for your company to survive, you need to make sure it runs smoothly and is stable. If you can lose real money on process failures, you need operation capabilities that prevent failures from happening or going undetected.

Contrasting Process Orchestration with Adjacent Technologies

The decision tree from Figure 61 should help you understand your requirements better. Still, you might be confused by tools or methods that also promise process automation in some form. How do they differ from a process orchestration platform? In this section, we'll explore some of the most common ones: RPA tools, data flow engines, event-driven architecture, data and event streaming technologies, BPMSs, and microservices orchestrators. Looking at the wider tooling landscape will also help refine your understanding of what process orchestration really is.

Robotic Process Automation (RPA)

RPA tools (such as UiPath) can automate tasks within legacy systems that don't provide any API. RPA is about screen scraping and simulating mouse or keyboard actions—kind of like the Microsoft Office macro recorder on steroids. It focuses on automating single tasks, not processes, but because the automation of a given task likely requires a series of interactions with the UI, which is typically represented in a graphical flow diagram, it often gets confused with process orchestration. The granularity of an RPA flow is very different from that of a business process, however, as discussed in the blog post "How to Benefit from Robotic Process Automation (RPA)."[108] You might quickly want to flip back to "Process Automation = Process Orchestration + Task Automation" starting on page 20 to refresh your memory on task automation vs. process orchestration.

Data Flow Engines and Data Streaming

There are technologies that can automate processes using a set of supposedly loosely coupled components. Most prominently this is about event-driven components, but data flow engines also fall into this category, as do traditional batch processing systems.

Let's look at data flow engines (e.g., Apache Airflow, Spring Cloud Data Flow), data streaming technologies, and ETL (extract-transform-load) tools first. There is one defining difference between these tools and a process orchestration platform: with process orchestration, there is an orchestrator that knows about and controls each instance of a process. You can think of the orchestrator as the conductor that drives the process. It keeps a list of all process instances, together with their current state. It always knows what has to come next in any given process instance. You can ask the orchestrator about the status of any process instance, and it can, for example, escalate the issue if something does not move forward as expected. In a nutshell, the process orchestrator maintains its own state so it knows exactly what is currently going on.

The situation is different with data flow engines or streaming architectures. They're steered by the data flowing through a pipeline. Very often, this follows a pattern where so-called *processors* take work from one place (e.g., a queue), do it, and place the result in another place (e.g., another queue), from which the next processor takes its work. The result is, of course, also a process, but the difference is that the data flow engine does not have its own state. There is no single component you can ask for information on the running instances and their state. Because of this different focus, these tools lack important features for process automation, such as support for control flow constructs like loops.

While in a process orchestrator you typically define the end-to-end process flow, you only define predecessors for processors in a data flow architecture. The resulting challenge with regard to the end process is that the process logic is pretty hidden. At the same time, the components are not as loosely coupled as it looks at first glance. The book *Practical Process Automation*[109] goes quite deeply into that topic if you are interested.

In summary, we don't see these tools as an alternative to a process orchestration platform, but rather as an addition that can be used for specific use cases. A good example use case for a combination of both technologies is where streams of data are used to generate insights that should lead to certain actions. This is described in the blog post "Event Streams Are Nothing Without Action."[110]

Event-Driven Architecture (EDA) and Event Streaming

In event-driven architectures, components react to events, which might be data in a stream. Those components don't know where this data is coming from. Common tooling includes event brokers like Apache Kafka.

A series of event subscriptions might form a logical chain that implements a business process. But this comes with two challenges. First, the process flow does not have its own persistence, making it hard to determine the current state of any instance. Second, the control flow logic isn't visible anywhere, making these architectures hard to understand and maintain. In essence, the problems are comparable to those described in the previous section.

If this is a discussion happening in your organization, we recommend picking up a copy of *Practical Process Automation*[111], which has a whole chapter on event-driven architecture (also known as choreography) versus process orchestration.

BPM Suites and Low-Code Application Platforms

There is a category of monolithic automation tools that also overlap with process orchestration platforms. Things start to get more nuanced here. The main tools in this category are traditional BPMSs and LCAPs. These tools approach process automation from a monolithic perspective, meaning they cannot easily be hooked into your own architecture. They typically come from big vendors in huge packages containing lots of adjacent automation features, making them complex to understand and use (especially because of their black-box nature). They are also often limited in scalability and as such may not be able to handle core business processes. Integrating endpoints into the process is done in a very proprietary way, meaning that special training is required to use these tools. Finally, they deliberately lock you into their environment instead of facilitating the use of best-of-breed solutions.

Microservice Orchestrators

Microservice orchestrators were invented with microservices in mind and focus fully on those architectures. As such, these tools don't cover the full scope required for end-to-end process orchestration. For example, human task management is not addressed, and legacy software and SaaS services that are not microservices aren't explicitly covered.

On top of this, these tools target solely software developers, which has a few notable consequences. First, the graphical representation of a process model is not considered important, so these tools miss out on the chance to align business and IT. This applies not only to the modeling itself, but also to process intelligence and process improvement. Second, the flow logic is typically kept deliberately simple—but as real-life processes are complex, this leads to a lot of complex workarounds being required, making the flow logic much harder to understand.

Tips on Evaluating Tools

We've found the following differentiators important when evaluating process automation and process orchestration tooling:

- **Support for end-to-end processes:** The tool should be able to orchestrate every human and automated task in an end-to-end business process across components such as systems, APIs, microservices, RPA bots, IoT devices, and AI/ML tools.

- **Support for long-running processes:** The tool should have the technical capabilities necessary to effectively manage business processes that run for hours, days, or even weeks. This is about effective persistence as well as querying possibilities and monitoring abilities.

- **Process-focused analytics and intelligence:** The tool should provide actionable insights based on real-time and historical process data, with features that help you optimize your processes.

- **Developer-friendliness:** The tool shouldn't require software developers to adopt a vendor-specific way of working, but instead should meet developers in their comfort zone. It should provide a good developer experience including powerful software development kits (SDKs) and getting started guides. Furthermore, the tool should ensure that you are not locked into a low-code layer, where you might hit barriers that you cannot overcome; allowing professional software development makes sure there is no wall you can hit. Finally, developer-friendliness is often also about the small things: having a vibrant community online, providing an open forum, or allowing problems to be solved with Google, Stack Overflow, or AI-powered CoPilot software.

- **Advanced workflow patterns:** Life is seldom a straight line, and the same is true of processes. Therefore, you must be able to accurately express all the things happening in your business processes for proper end-to-end process orchestration. This requires workflow patterns that go beyond basic control flow patterns (like sequences or conditions). If your orchestration tool does not provide those advanced workflow patterns, your developers will need to implement time-consuming workarounds, and you will end up with confusing models. This is explored further in the blog post "Why Process Orchestration Needs Advanced Workflow Patterns."[112]

- **Standards-based collaboration:** The tool should use open standards (namely BPMN and DMN) to facilitate communication and alignment between business stakeholders and IT teams.

- **Flexible architecture:** The tool should allow teams to choose which parts to use and where, integrate seamlessly with other IT tools, and offer on-premise, cloud, and hybrid deployment options.

- **Open architecture:** The tool should provide open APIs for integration, allow teams to try it before adopting it, and support community-driven extension and improvement.

- **Low total cost of ownership:** The tool should enable organizations to get started quickly and to make changes easily, with no proprietary or vendor-specific knowledge required.

- **Scalability and resilience:** The tool should be built to align with modern cloud engineering practices to support cloud-first process automation initiatives that can scale horizontally. Supporting a proper level of scaling is important to handle increasing load, whether seasonal or due to overall business success. You need to have a platform that supports whatever your business requires. This will allow you to apply process orchestration to a bigger variety of processes, including core processes running huge loads (like payments or trade processing). To guarantee high availability for your processes, you'll also need to ensure a high level of resilience and HA, as discussed in "Resilience and High Availability" starting on page 136.

It's important to have clarity on what kind of tool you need, as tool categories around process automation, process orchestration, task automation, and integration are blurry. This does not make it easy to select the right tool stack, but hopefully the information in this book will help you make better decisions. The following are some of the key points to keep in mind:

1. Using standard (COTS) software can be the easiest and cheapest way to automate processes. Note, however, that you won't be able to differentiate yourself by those processes, and you will have to adjust your organization's way of working to the software, not the other way around. For all processes that require a tailor-made process orchestration solution, standard software can be one piece of the puzzle, but it won't be sufficient on its own.

2. Task automation tools (including iPaaS and RPA tools) cannot replace process orchestration, but they can complement a process orchestration platform for specific task automations.

3. Data streaming or event-driven approaches distribute and hide the flow logic, making those bad choices to automate important business processes. There are use cases where those tools are a great choice, though, and use cases where a combination of process orchestration and data or event streaming will work well.

4. BMPSs and LCAPs have some overlap with process orchestration platforms, but they're typically not flexible or developer-friendly and don't have the open architecture required to orchestrate all your processes strategically.

5. Microservice orchestrators are too technical for business processes, lacking features to align business and IT and also typically lacking extended workflow patterns to support all the complexities of core processes.

Ideally, you'll get help when selecting your tool stack. This could mean involving external consultancies or analysts. This decision is vital for the future of your transformation initiative; technology isn't everything, but such transformations can easily get stalled by improper tool choices. The selected tool needs to be able to support your strategy.

Run early proof of concept sessions, and let your own employees be part of these. Don't leave the whole decision process in the hands of external stakeholders, as this will not only leave you with limited knowledge of the reasoning behind the choice but can also lead to more short-sighted decisions.

Questions to Assess Your Maturity

For technology, we describe the five maturity levels as follows (see Figure 3):

- Level 1: Teams may have implemented disparate automation technologies.
- Level 2: Teams are questioning the continued use of legacy systems or monolithic on-premise solutions that limit advancement.
- Level 3: The focus is on building a single technology stack that covers the entire process lifecycle.
- Level 4: Investing in elements that increase solution acceleration, with a focus on enabling multiple teams to build process orchestration solutions at scale.
- Level 5: Recognizing that there is no "one-size-fits-all" approach to hyperautomated tech stacks, the organization has instead built one that fits its exact needs; it also has a dedicated process orchestration strategy within the stack.

Questions you should ask yourself to assess your maturity include:

- Do you have a high-level vision of your enterprise architecture around process orchestration, including technical and business capabilities and end-to-end processes?
- Do you have the technical capabilities identified in your enterprise architecture, and have you selected a tool stack that can implement those capabilities?
- Do you have a clear understanding of why this tool stack was chosen and how it's differentiated from competing categories or tools (in case other parts of the organization challenge your decision)?
- Do you provide the important technical capabilities around process orchestration as a platform within the organization?
- Is this platform operated in a SaaS-like way to ease usage for delivery teams?
- Do you have enablement around that platform?
- Do you provide accelerators and reusable components around that platform?
- Do you have best practices on how different domains, teams, and solutions can leverage that platform (like multitenancy and sizing)?
- Do you have enough internal marketing and communications to make people aware of process orchestration and how to approach it?

Part IV: Delivery

Having shaped a great vision, set up a rockstar team, defined a great architecture, and decided on your tool stack leaves you with the most important part of your process orchestration journey still ahead of you: creating concrete orchestration solutions that deliver real value for your organization. So far, everything you've done was kind of a warm-up, with no direct business value contribution delivered just yet. But if you've done all that work well, the solution delivery should run smoothly.

In this chapter, we'll describe the typical steps and iterations involved in developing one concrete solution. Of course, this is also interlinked with architecture work and tool selection, so during your first projects you will typically define and refine your overall architecture and best practices. Only after you've completed those first projects will you be able to scale your solution creation efforts.

Solution Creation Approach

Most often, we see approaches similar to the one sketched out in Figure 62. Of course, even though the approach shown in this visual appears to follow a straight line, that is almost never the case in real life; solutions are best created in an agile fashion, continuously delivering business value in small iterations, and not by following rigid waterfall models.

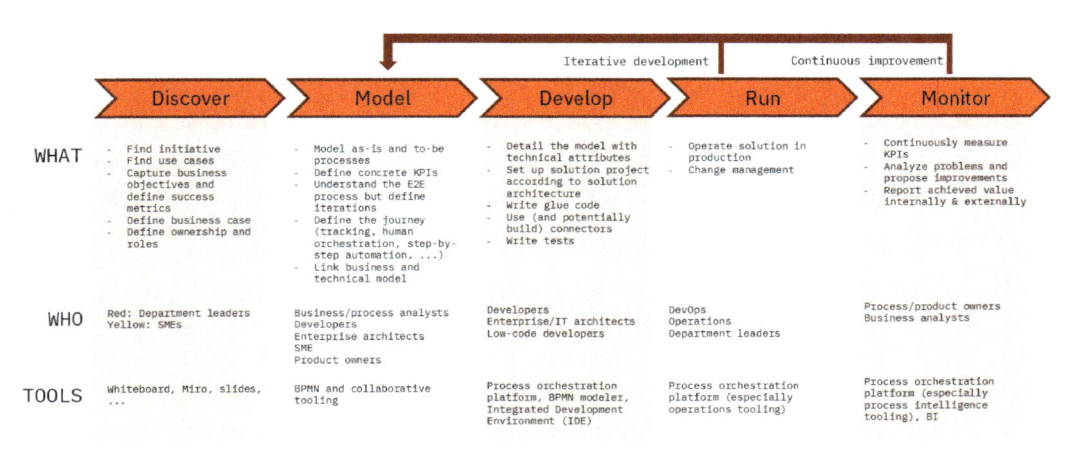

	Discover	Model	Develop	Run	Monitor
WHAT	- Find initiative - Find use cases - Capture business objectives and define success metrics - Define business case - Define ownership and roles	- Model as-is and to-be processes - Define concrete KPIs - Understand the E2E process but define iterations - Define the journey (tracking, human orchestration, step-by-step automation, ...) - Link business and technical model	- Detail the model with technical attributes - Set up solution project according to solution architecture - Write glue code - Use (and potentially build) connectors - Write tests	- Operate solution in production - Change management	- Continuously measure KPIs - Analyze problems and propose improvements - Report achieved value internally & externally
WHO	Red: Department leaders Yellow: SMEs	Business/process analysts Developers Enterprise architects SME Product owners	Developers Enterprise/IT architects Low-code developers	DevOps Operations Department leaders	Process/product owners Business analysts
TOOLS	Whiteboard, Miro, slides, ...	BPMN and collaborative tooling	Process orchestration platform, BPMN modeler, Integrated Development Environment (IDE)	Process orchestration platform (especially operations tooling)	Process orchestration platform (especially process intelligence tooling), BI

(Iterative development: Model → Develop → Run. Continuous improvement: Run → Monitor.)

Figure 62: The solution creation lifecycle

149

Note that we also advise adopting product thinking in your organization, as discussed in "Product Thinking" starting on page 65. This means you want to have stable and long-lasting ownership for every solution, even if the solution is created or improved by dedicated projects. This allows the respective owner to think strategically about the solution.

Let's go through the various steps in the solution creation approach one by one.

Discover

Very often, this step is not really part of a solution project, as typically you have to evaluate process candidates for orchestration and consider the resulting business case first, in order to come up with concrete next projects.

The aims of the discovery phase are to:

- **Identify a process to orchestrate** and define the **business case** for the automation project.
- **Capture business objectives and define success metrics.** It should be clear not only why a process should be automated, but which metrics will define success. These could be, for example, around cycle times, reduced amount of human work, or increased sales through better customer experiences. In our experience, this step is often overlooked, which not only makes it hard to communicate value later but also misses an opportunity to align everyone on a common goal.
- **Define ownership and roles.** Before kicking off your solution, it's crucial to understand how it is connected with the business domains that are holding the use case together (we advocate for clear process ownership) and the roles and enablement that are needed to deliver the initiative.

Model

Model the to-be process to a high standard. The model you create should be clear, understandable, and precise, as it will be the basis for the executable process. Although the primary focus should of course be on the to-be process, as this is where value will come from, it's often helpful to capture the as-is process first, to better understand the changes needed to implement the new process.

While you should aim to get a clear understanding of the end-to-end process, in the early phases of your project you can limit that to a higher level of abstraction and only define the next iteration of your orchestration project in detail. For example, you might start with the happy path and not yet go into all exceptional paths or define all the technical details around the APIs required for the whole process. The end-to-end view is still important for the context, however, and it will help you define the iterations.

When you define your to-be process model for the next development iteration, make sure to start developing as soon as possible to allow for quick feedback cycles. Your first process models might not be suitable directly for execution, but most organizations will get better at this very quickly, especially if they have teams consisting of business people, BPMN experts, and IT folks.

A common topic of discussion is the link between business and technical process models. We've heard a lot of misguided comments in this area, and to shape the discussion we recommend taking a look at the "Camunda house," discussed in detail in *Real-Life BPMN*[113] (see Figure 63). The house differentiates a strategic process model, which is a very simplified overview of a process that typically fits on one slide, and the operational model, which is logically correct and directly executable. It contains everything required for a process orchestration engine to do its work.

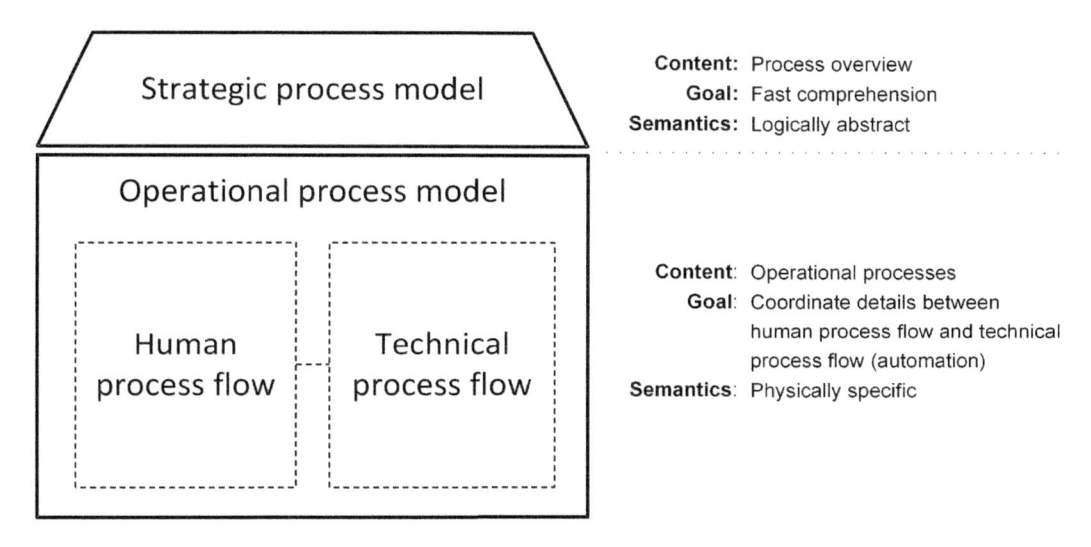

Figure 63: The Camunda process house from the book "Real-Life BPMN"

The strategic model is a model purely expressing the "why" of a process on a business level, without too many operational details, whereas the operational model is a shared model between business and IT. This is exactly the power of BPMN: you do not need two disconnected models for business and IT, but rather can have one joined operational model.

Of course, you might end up with multiple physical copies of that model: for example, one in the collaborative modeling tool, one in the company-internal wiki, and one in the version control of the IT solution. This is completely fine, and we will describe steps you can take to keep those models in sync later in this chapter.

Develop

Next up is the development of the solution, which means adding all the technical details needed to make a process model executable. For example, this can involve expressions to implement decision points (gateways), glue code to integrate service calls, configuration of connectors (or the implementation of your own connectors), and user interfaces (including task forms). Development should also include writing automated tests, at least for solutions with a certain level of criticality.

Depending on the process at hand, the development phase might involve more pro-code or low-code elements. We will describe the development of solutions at both ends of the spectrum in more detail later in this chapter.

Run

The solution will only generate business value once it's running production. This phase includes setting up the real deployment environment, even if this is hopefully handled as a service by either your SaaS vendor or your internal CoE. Also, before putting your solution into production it's important to consider change management for the people who will be affected, for example because they'll need to switch to using the new task management UI or otherwise change the way they do their work.

The delivery team needs to technically operate the solution and watch for any incidents that might happen. Most customers have a two-layered approach to this. IT runs technical operations, perhaps with someone on-call (often 24/7, depending on the criticality of the process). If you have a platform as a service in-house, those people are typically connected to your CoE and should resolve failures in the underlying platform themselves. Sometimes solution teams operate their own platforms, in which case they typically resolve those problems. In the meantime, anything that happens in the application and process layer is normally forwarded to the operations part of the delivery team. This might include failures that occur if process instances get stuck because of invalid data or bugs, for example.

As soon as the first iteration is in production, you can immediately begin implementing the next iteration, making improvements or simply implementing the next process phase.

Monitor

Once in production, you should **continuously track value**. Make sure you implement automatic capturing of the KPIs you defined at the start of the project, probably via the process intelligence tool. The process orchestration platform will help you to automatically capture all relevant data and provide real-time dashboards for executives.

Once your process is in production, you should also continuously check for improvement ideas. In our experience, once process owners have visibility on their process's KPIs they can often quickly and easily identify low-hanging fruit for improvement. If you establish a product mindset around your processes, they will be incentivized to act on those insights, and the visual process model makes it easy to implement such changes.

Setting the Stage for Success: Your Early Projects

We deliberately left out the first projects in Figure 62 for simplicity's sake—but of course, your first process orchestration projects are something special. Typically, those first solutions will be developed hand-in-hand with shaping your architecture and selecting your tools. Ideally, a stable team of people will be involved with the first projects, and those folks will then also be involved building the CoE (or the other way around: your CoE may actually be doing the implementation work for the first projects in order to establish the architecture).

Avoid defining too much of a platform without running a concrete project, as this bears the risk of getting into an ivory tower situation that doesn't deliver what people really need.

The most important additional steps for your first projects are:

- Defining your stack and selecting your tool(s)
- Defining your solution design
- Piloting your architecture (you'll continue to validate and improve it in later projects)
- Documenting lessons learned
- Creating enablement material

As part of the tool selection process, we recommend doing proofs of concept early on, as only those can prove that a tool is working for you—something a spreadsheet with evaluation criteria cannot!

In a PoC, you need to model the process with the goal of the PoC in mind. You likely won't need to model the full process, but can concentrate on specific tasks, such as calling real services in your environment, or executing human tasks if appropriate. You might use existing tools from the vendor (e.g., Camunda Tasklist) as a first step to save effort in developing your own tasklist, unless a tasklist is important for your overall proof. Include some "eye candy," like reporting, to make non-technical stakeholders happy. The PoC should convey the value of process orchestration to the organization. However, concentrate on just the important aspects to do the proof, and be prepared to throw away the code afterward and start fresh for the pilot (it's perfectly valid for early PoCs to be "hacky" in order to keep the focus on the end goals). See Camunda's best practice guide to doing a proper PoC[114] for more information on this topic.

In general, the early projects often serve as lighthouses and may provide a copy-and-paste template for later projects. Hence, it's important to review those projects after they've gone live. Because of the lighthouse effect, it's worth putting in some extra effort to clean them up. It's better to plan time for this after the go-live than to try to make things perfect during early development, as you will have learned a lot by the time the pilot has been running on the live system for a while.

Try to avoid doing too many projects in parallel at the beginning, to allow new learning to influence your future work. If you have parallel pilots, organize knowledge sharing between the teams. Ideally, have the team working on the first pilot implement the next orchestration solution.

Typical Delivery Teams and Roles

At this point, we'd like to revisit the question of what people, roles, and skills you need in your delivery teams. Guess what? It depends! The most important factor is the type of solution you are building. A pro-code approach requires a different setup than a more low-code one, so let's look at those separately.

For *pro-code solutions*, a delivery team requires at least a software developer and a business analyst (for a refresher on how we define these roles, see "Roles" starting on page 76). Very often, you will also see other roles in the team: solution architects, Scrum masters, test engineers, DevOps engineers, methodology experts (e.g., around BPMN), etc. The exact team composition that's appropriate will depend on your way of developing software. In other words, you will see normal software development teams, but with added process orchestration experience. This experience can be achieved by training or enablement.

From a process orchestration perspective, the important aspect is that at least software developers and solution architects need to be trained in BPMN and the process orchestration platform. A CoE can either provide full-time team members with the required training or supply part-time team members to help with these tasks as needed. The latter approach is especially useful for very specific skills, for example around modeling complex scenarios in BPMN or tuning the performance of the process orchestration platform.

For *low-code solutions*, on the other hand, you don't always find software engineers in the delivery teams. This is possible because the complexity of the solutions is lower. In this case, the CoE likely provides supporting artifacts like bespoke connectors optimized for internal use in the organization. This removes the necessity for delivery teams to have engineering expertise themselves. However, expertise around process orchestration and BPMN is still required; again, this can be achieved by training or enablement from the CoE.

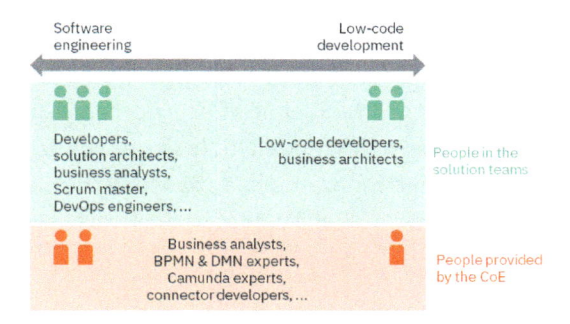

Figure 64: Possible compositions of delivery teams

One very important aspect is that the business must be represented in all delivery projects. This generally happens on two levels: operationally and strategically (as pointed out in "Part 1: Vision" starting on page 39). On an operational level, you will need business analysts or subject matter experts that provide concrete input on how to orchestrate the process, dealing with day-to-day requirements. On a strategic level, you need somebody—often also from the CoE—that can connect to business executives, gather their input, understand their priorities, and explain the business value to them. This is a point of failure we often see, as business analysts and business architects do not always speak the language of executives. This role should be filled by someone who really understands the opportunities that technology provides to the business and knows how to capture that and make it transparent to leadership. This is often a central role. In CoEs, the task of creating initial awareness within the business is commonly taken on by the CoE lead; solution architects then navigate the business domains along the process development lifecycle, from discovery to modeling, monitoring, and improving.

Solution Design

Let's get into the weeds of how to design a process solution using process orchestration and process models in BPMN. We'll start by describing the greenfield architecture Camunda has defined for its customers (using a concrete tool makes this section much more hands-on; if you use other tools, you should still be able to draw value from it).

We differentiate two flavors of the greenfield architecture:

- Greenfield architecture for pro-code (red, using the categories from "A Useful Categorization of Use Cases" starting on page 33) use cases
- Simplified architecture for low-code (yellow) use cases

Of course, the boundary between red and yellow use cases is blurry (see "A Useful Categorization of Use Cases" starting on page 33). There might, for example, be use cases where 90% of the solution creation is yellow, but a small part of the orchestration process requires custom-implemented code—and for governance reasons, that also means that the overall build and deployment happens via a defined CI/CD pipeline after automated unit tests are run, even if many changes might only affect the BPMN model. In this case, you could tailor your software development lifecycle (SDLC) so that, for example, a change in the process model made by a business persona in your collaborative modeling environment also triggers the deployment pipeline.

This is not only possible, but actually a great enabler, as it allows working in a low-code fashion but still can guarantee a high level of quality. In Camunda's case, all the tools in the stack have an API, so you could, for example, pull BPMN models from a milestone in the web modeler and push them to Git automatically on changes or during deployment.

Of course, design and architecture depend on hundreds of things, so you'll likely need to adjust the solution design proposals in this book to your own needs. Our goal here is simply to provide a sensible default that's a good starting point and has been validated in many situations. This can be quite useful to have when you're getting started with your first project, and you need to make a lot of decisions but still lack firsthand experience!

Many of our customers start with this proposal and adjust it to their organization's needs over time (Camunda leaves a lot of flexibility for this). Those adjusted defaults might then be rolled out through the organization, with the help of the CoE.

Greenfield Solution Architecture for Pro-Code Use Cases

Let's explore the solution design and development scenario for red use cases first. Remember, these are your most complex and critical processes, which will be implemented using proven industry best practices around software engineering. This helps ensure that you will create high-quality solutions that can be continuously improved over time.

Typically, the process orchestration solution will look something like what you see in Figure 65. The exact technologies used will depend on your organization's preferences, so, for example, if you're a Java shop you might want to create a Maven project using Spring Boot and the Camunda Spring SDK[115], and if you're a .NET shop you will likely prefer C# and the Camunda C# Client[116] as a NuGet package. (For more technical details, see our best practice guide to deciding about your stack[117].)

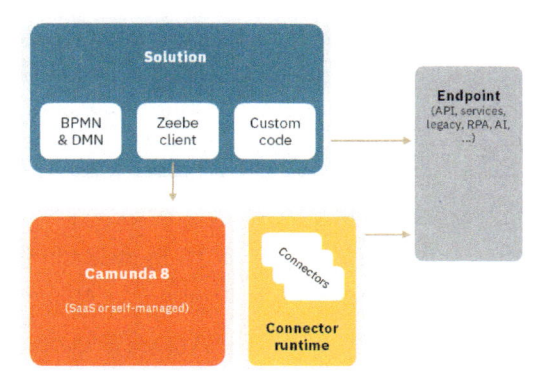

Figure 65: The greenfield solution architecture for pro-code use cases

A solution contains your process or decision models (as BPMN or DMN files), your own code, and the client SDK (as a library) to connect to Camunda. To integrate endpoints, you can either write custom glue code or use existing connectors. The solution should also contain automated unit tests (like JUnit tests in Java)—you can find more information on this in Camunda's best practice guide to testing process definitions[118].

The solution is built via your preferred CI/CD pipeline (e.g., GitHub and GitHub Actions, or Jenkins). This results in a normal deployment artifact (e.g., a Spring Boot JAR) that is deployed into your normal runtime environment (e.g., Kubernetes via Docker images). The BPMN and DMN models will be part of that artifact, and they're deployed to Camunda during startup of the application.

The Software Development Lifecycle and Model Roundtrips

While the solution architecture looks surprisingly similar for most solutions, the way to get the BPMN model in there differs. Most lifecycles start within a collaborative web modeling tool like Camunda Web Modeler[119]. There are two reasons for this:

1. The web modeler brings collaborative features to the table. Especially during early discussions around the business process, using the web modeler makes sure that you can involve all important stakeholders, independent of their role. This facilitates discussions about the process model. Also, the model can be easily hooked into company-internal wikis. Hence, in many organizations, the web modeler is an important collaboration tool that facilitates the process mindset.

2. The web modeler has a low barrier to entry. You can create your first process model right away, without thinking about version control structures or anything else you need to set up. Typically, you will just create a project folder for your first models; we recommend not worrying about default structures or guidelines for the moment, as this first phase is really just about getting started.

However, solutions will not be solely developed within the web modeler. After this initial stage the model needs to be put into a development project (e.g., in Git). This offers the following benefits:

- You can write unit tests that run completely locally, accessing the model locally in the developer's filesystem.
- You can set up a CI/CD pipeline that has the process model included, so it can also run unit tests and create a unified artifact containing all relevant elements of the process solution.
- You can tag and release solutions, including the process model and all other code artifacts around it.
- You can use a local Camunda platform for development, enabling a completely offline developer experience.

Developers typically prefer using a desktop tool (e.g., Camunda Desktop Modeler[120]) to edit the local files. Of course, with this development approach, you will end up with multiple physical copies of your process model: one in the web modeler's repository, and one in the developer's version control system. This requires thinking about keeping those models in sync, which necessitates a roundtrip from one system to the other—the business creates the model, and the developer alters the model in their own environment and syncs it back with the business model. One possibility (the one we see most often in practice) is to use CLI tools[121] to handle the synchronization process, which is triggered manually by the developer. Another possibility is to use the web modeler's API to automatically sync changes back and forth, although this carries some risk of changes being overwritten accidentally.

With that background in mind, let's look at a typical journey, as illustrated in Figure 66, concentrating solely on the tools and ignoring which roles are doing what for now.

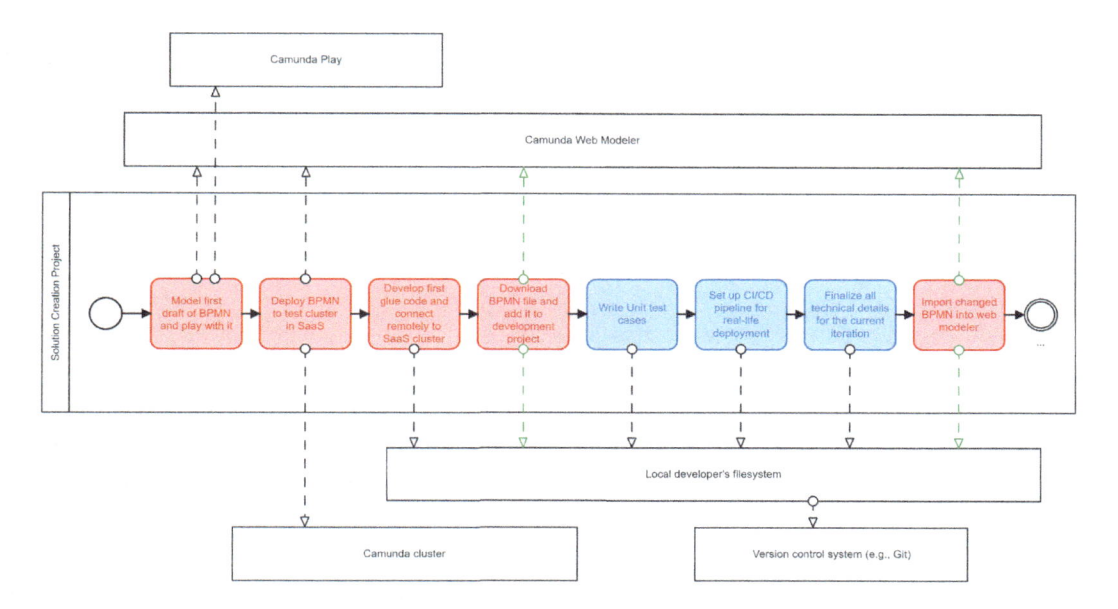

Figure 66: An example journey (aka roundtrip) to create an executable BPMN model through the various Camunda tools

Let's quickly go through this. First, either a developer or a business analyst sketches the initial version of the BPMN process model to be executed. Using the web modeler lowers the barriers to just start modeling and allows you to involve as many people as possible in this process. The model can be directly deployed to a test cluster in Camunda SaaS, and the Camunda Web Modeler's Play mode can be used to test drive the model in order to improve it.

When service tasks need to integrate systems, either out-of-the-box connectors are used or a development project is created (using tools like Java, Maven, Spring Boot, and Git). In the first step, you might keep using a test cluster in Camunda SaaS and just add API credentials to access it from the developer's machine. In PoC situations, this approach lets you get started quickly, and keeping the model in the web modeler for as long as possible allows you to easily discuss it with all stakeholders.

At some point in time, though, you'll want to move the model into the developer's filesystem, so you can start writing unit tests and create your CI/CD pipeline, or simply because you want to run everything locally on the developer's machine. In Camunda Web Modeler, downloading the model is currently a manual step using the download button (but a feature to automate this step is on the roadmap).

Whenever changes are made to the developer's copy of the model, the model should be copied back to the web modeler to avoid those models diverging. This is done by manually importing the BPMN file into the web modeler (a feature to automate this step is also on the roadmap).

Many projects institutionalize the process for keeping the different versions in sync as part of their development process—for example, when using Scrum this can be done as part of the planning or retrospective sessions. It can also be part of the definition of done (DoD) for development issues.

Simplified Solution Architecture for Low-Code Use Cases

Simpler process solutions—yellow processes, in our categorization—might not require the full-blown software development setup described above. For such cases, it's often preferable to use a simplified solution architecture that's more accessible to non-software developers. These solutions might not contain dedicated programming code, but just process models, decision models, and forms. Those can be designed using a web-based modeler like Camunda's, so the creator doesn't need any locally installed tools. If a solution requires custom code, for example to connect to the organization's internal legacy system, the CoE can develop this code and provide it to the solution creator as a reusable connector, to avoid the solution turning into a development project. This is visualized in Figure 67.

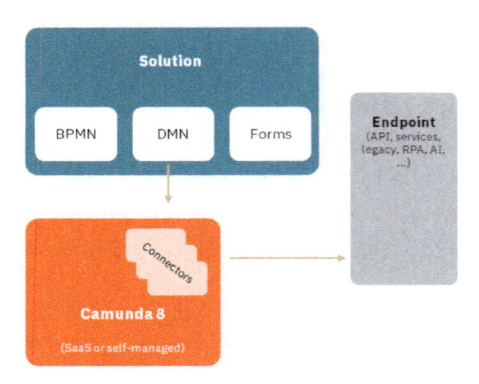

Figure 67: A simplified solution architecture for low-code use cases that don't need developer tools

There are two ways to deploy such a solution:

1. Deploy manually via a button in the web modeler. While this is easy and straightforward, it lacks any kind of quality assurance or controls.

2. Create a milestone and use milestones to trigger a deployment pipeline in your CI tool[122] (e.g., GitHub Actions). This approach provides a good balance between ease of use and quality, but requires your organization to set up those pipelines initially.

At Camunda, we are currently working on improving our low-code experience, so please reach out if you have questions, feedback, or simply want to discuss your vision of the best lifecycle for low-code solutions.

Typical Questions Around the Development Lifecycle

In this section, we'll address some of the questions that commonly arise around the development lifecycle. First, though, one important note. We have learned over the last decade that roles vary widely across enterprises, not only in their responsibilities but also in what they're called. The same responsibilities can be assigned to roles with different names, and roles that have the same name can have completely different responsibilities. And of course, each person fulfilling a role will perform it in their own way. What's more, in smaller projects, one person might take on several (or even all) of the roles we discussed here. That's all OK, but please keep in mind that when giving the following answers we focus on what in our experience is a "typical" scenario.

When does the business analyst stop modeling and developers take over?

The typical approach goes as follows: business analysts, focusing on the requirements and the communication to stakeholders, typically create the first draft of a model. They should of course have an executable process model in mind, but they might make some mistakes. Ideally, the business analyst collaborates with developers as well as end users to make sure they develop a model that will, later on, be executable. The best situations we have seen are workshops with all those roles together in one room discussing the model. In such a setting, the business analysts might, for example, learn why it is hard to implement a process in the current IT ecosystem, and the developers might learn that legal requirements are what led to such a complicated process. These insights alone have huge value.

Keep in mind that you should not try to sketch a perfect model right away. Most often, it is better to focus on a minimal viable product (MVP) first and make this process model executable going through the whole lifecycle. This helps everybody in the team to understand how things really work, which in turn will ensure the team knows how to create good models when moving forward.

This MVP model is handed over to developers to add all the technical details required to make it executable.

What happens if the business analyst needs to make changes later on?

As described previously, you might work on two physical copies of the model: one in the developer's version control and one in the web modeler. It's important to have clarity on which model is leading, when a business analyst can make changes to the web modeler, and how changes are merged.

Most often, we see defined points in time where those merges happen. So, the business analyst can make changes in the web modeler and add those changes to a user story to implement (e.g., using the web modeler's diffing features). Those changes are then either merged using an XML merge tool or simply remodeled in the desktop modeler (again, more features for this are on Camunda's roadmap).

How do you improve currently deployed processes, and who drives those improvements?

The currently deployed process should have found its way back into the web modeler too, and you can discuss changes there to arrive at a concrete improvement story, which will then be merged into or remodeled in the executable process model. In general, we have found that while remodeling is not very attractive to many people, it's a simple approach that works pretty well, as the actual changes that need to be made to the model are typically small compared to the volume of the discussions that go into them. Diffing features in the modeling tools can help you identify the relevant changes.

Most often, in pro-code scenarios, there are subsequent changes based on process changes anyway; for example, test cases might need to be altered or data mappings might need to be adjusted. Those changes are driven by the developer, so it makes sense that the same person also does the model changes.

How are models marked as ready for production?

In pro-code scenarios, you use the same mechanisms as for source code, meaning that you tag code in your version control system and run whatever testing and QA procedure you require, and this leads to changes being pushed to production.

While models allow for a shortcut (deploying changed models to production during runtime via an API), we advise against using those shortcuts in most scenarios to make sure you maintain the governance you need for red use cases. Of course, there might be exceptions to this rule; for example, you might allow certain DMN tables to be adjusted by business roles on the fly without QA. You need to make a conscious decision in such cases, keeping in mind the risks of such shortcuts.

How do I prevent unauthorized changes?

Typically, authorization is applied on a version control level, meaning only the developers can make changes to the process models used in production. Access to process models in the web modeler is typically rather liberal, as there is value in many people collaborating. Using the milestone feature, the process owner can make sure to control what's going on and potentially roll back changes.

Does the approach change with the maturity of the organization?

The more mature an organization is, the more standardization typically happens around the solution architecture and project templates. This makes it easier to quickly start a development project, which might reduce the web modeler's role in that respect, but its role for collaboration is still the same.

Who brings the developed models to production? Which parts of this can be done without IT involvement?

In red use cases, models are deployed to production by the production application itself, which is in turn deployed by your CI/CD pipeline. Assuming that this pipeline is automated, you do not need IT to trigger it. So, while most often developers will push changes to version control and create the appropriate tags to trigger a deployment, you could also trigger that by new milestones in the web modeler created by business people.

Now we enter a scale of less IT involvement that goes as far as doing deployments from the web modeler manually, which can be done without any IT involvement at all.

The approach that is appropriate for you to take depends on your situation, taking into account the roles involved, the maturity of your organization, and also the complexity and non-functional requirements of the orchestration solution.

Accelerating Solution Building

In essence, there are two options for accelerating projects:

1. **Use vendor-provided accelerators:** Use components that are shipped with your vendor's product or which are available via its ecosystem. The prime examples are out-of-the-box connectors that can be used directly, but solution templates or process blueprints might also speed up your projects.

2. **Build your own accelerators within the organization:** Another very successful way to speed up your projects is to build components yourself that can be reused in various projects. A central function like the CoE can build and own such components, and all federated solutions can make use of them.

Let's dive into the example of custom connectors, as they are a great way to make certain bespoke logic reusable across the organization. These connectors need to be maintained as well as operated. Typically, every connector is created and maintained as its own development project, somewhere in your version control system. This is in line with what we do for Camunda's own connectors[123]. Every connector should have a clear owner, which might be the CoE itself, or some team that originally developed the connector.

How the connector is operated is an interesting question. Generally, one or more connectors can be bundled together into a connector runtime, as you can find in Camunda's out-of-the-box connector bundle[124]. The connector bundle is a Java application or Docker image that needs to be run for every Camunda cluster that wants to make use of those connectors.

If you run Camunda self-managed, then you might simply add your custom connector bundle to your Helm charts to be created with every cluster. If you run Camunda SaaS, you run the connector bundle yourself, connecting to SaaS via API credentials.

Some customers run multiple connector bundles to satisfy different non-functional requirements. For example, some connectors might need to be co-located with the system they connect to, which also allows hybrid cloud scenarios. This removes the burden of requiring firewall access to the system (instead, the connector polls for work); it also allows credentials to stay out of the process orchestration platform's context, and it means sensitive data might never leave your network at all. You might also want to separate connectors that need to scale massively or that are particularly critical from others.

Of course, as mentioned above, acceleration is not limited to connectors. Other components that can be reused to speed up projects include:

- Solution templates (e.g., Maven archetypes) and reference architectures
- Process blueprints
- Testing frameworks (especially testing mechanisms close to the business, like behavior-driven development [BDD])
- Modular business capabilities (see "Enterprise Architecture: A High-Level View" starting on page 110)
- Forms

Change Management

The successful deployment of a new process solution is not only a technical endeavor; it is most often also a transformative journey that requires careful consideration of organizational change management. This is because the deployment might disrupt existing workflows, tasks, roles, and responsibilities within an organization. Without effective change management, resistance, uncertainty, and fear can impede the adoption and success of the new automation solution. Therefore, it is essential that change management not be an afterthought, but an integral part of the deployment process.

We often see Dr. John Kotter's 8-Step Process for Leading Change[125] applied in this context. It guides organizations through the following stages:

1. Create a sense of urgency

2. Build a guiding coalition
3. Form a vision and strategy
4. Enlist a volunteer army
5. Enable action by removing barriers
6. Generate short-term wins
7. Sustain acceleration
8. Institute change

Suppose, for example, a bank (let's call it "Flow Bank" for the sake of this story) is grappling with an increasingly cumbersome onboarding process. Clerks spend countless hours navigating through piles of documents and exchanging numerous emails to complete the necessary steps to fulfill all the regulatory requirements and add customers to all the necessary backend systems. The bank decides to replace this with an orchestrated onboarding process that involves a human whenever necessary via a tasklist user interface, and routes all required information properly to the right person at the right time. Several steps of the onboarding process will be automated right away, but essentially the orchestration solution should be the first step in an iterative process to increase automation step by step.

Let's look at how Kotter's process could work in this case, focusing on the back office employees. Charlie, the bank's chief operations officer, is leading this change personally:

1. **Create a sense of urgency.** Charlie highlights the growing frustration among clerks and clients due to the inefficiencies in the current onboarding process. They emphasize the competitive landscape and the need for Flow Bank to deliver a seamless and efficient experience to clients from the outset or risk losing a significant part of its market share in the next few years, creating a sense of urgency among the team.

2. **Build a guiding coalition.** Charlie assembles a coalition comprising department heads, IT specialists, compliance officers, and frontline employees. Together, they form a cohesive team committed to driving the change and ensuring its successful implementation. This team is involved in the solution creation and knows what the new orchestrated process will look like.

3. **Form a vision and strategy.** The coalition collaborates to develop a clear vision for the onboarding transformation: to leverage a new system that will digitize and automate the onboarding process, reducing manual effort and enhancing the client experience. At the same time, it will remove internal friction and automate some tedious tasks, thus making work less annoying for the people involved. They outline a strategy, including not only the solution creation but also training staff and managing the transition.

4. **Enlist a volunteer army (by communicating the vision).** Charlie and the coalition communicate the vision and benefits of the new system to the entire organization through town hall meetings, departmental briefings, and regular updates. They emphasize how the streamlined onboarding process will improve efficiency, accuracy, and client satisfaction.

5. **Enable action by removing barriers.** To empower the broad-based action, Charlie organizes comprehensive training sessions on the new system, tailored to different roles and responsibilities. They encourage open dialogue, soliciting feedback and addressing concerns to ensure a smooth transition for all stakeholders.

6. **Generate short-term wins.** As the new process solution is rolled out, Charlie celebrates early successes and milestones achieved. They highlight stories of clerks who have adapted quickly to the new system, showcasing its benefits and inspiring others to embrace change. They also measure the faster cycle times and report on how quickly customers can now open a bank account.

7. **Sustain acceleration (by consolidating gains and producing more change).** Building on initial successes, Charlie and the coalition continue to refine the onboarding system, incorporating feedback and making enhancements based on user experiences. They expand the system's capabilities and further streamline and automate processes and improve efficiency.

8. **Institute change (by anchoring the new approach in the culture).** Over time, the new onboarding process becomes ingrained in Flow Bank's culture, transforming the way frontline employees interact with clients and each other. Through ongoing training, reinforcement, and recognition of employees' efforts, Charlie ensures that the change becomes a permanent fixture, driving sustained improvement and innovation.

In the end, Charlie's commitment to Kotter's 8-Step Process for Leading Change enabled Flow Bank to successfully introduce the new onboarding process, revolutionizing its operations and allowing it to deliver a seamless and streamlined experience to clients that set the bank apart in the competitive financial landscape.

We hope that this hypothetical example can serve as inspiration for you in implementing your own change management practices.

Questions to Assess Your Maturity

For delivery, we describe the five maturity levels as follows (see Figure 3):

- Level 1: Large gaps between business and IT create silos, leading to slow iterations and limited ability to deliver impactful process solutions.
- Level 2: Business starts to recognize the transformational potential of IT, but lack of mature IT methodologies prevents agile delivery in small increments.

- Level 3: As business and IT alignment improves and the organization shifts to more agile development, teams begin to deliver continuous improvements in short sprints based on process data.
- Level 4: Multiple BizDevOps teams are involved in delivery and establishing best practices that speed up time to value; improved process monitoring allows organizations to track impact on business outcomes.
- Level 5: Business teams can self-serve on an increasing number of use cases with minimal IT involvement, enabled by the CoE; processes are purpose-built to drive business value and adjusted through continuous monitoring and improvement to maximize value.

Questions you should ask yourself to assess your maturity include:

- How closely are business and IT teams collaborating to deliver process solutions?
- Do you have a standardized business case creation process that defines tangible success outcomes?
- Are your delivery teams using iterative development and continuous improvement approaches, to deliver value incrementally?
- Are you systematically tracking the achieved business value of your delivery initiatives?
- How many delivery teams do you have in your organization that are actively working on process orchestration solutions?
- How do you accelerate solution building through reusable components?
- Have you enabled yellow (medium-complexity) use cases to work with as little IT involvement as possible (e.g., by providing connectors)?

Part V: Measurement

Define Metrics and Key Performance Indicators (KPIs)

Evaluate Metrics

Continuously Communicate Value

Questions to Assess Your Maturity

For technology, we describe the five maturity levels as follows:

- Level 1: ...
- Level 2: ...
- Level 3: ...
- Level 4: ...
- Level 5: ...

Questions you should ask yourself to assess your maturity include:

- xxx

Closing Thoughts

Continuously Monitor and Improve Your Maturity Level

Further Resources

Where to Get Help

Get Going!

References

[1] mailto:bernd.ruecker@camunda.com

[2] mailto:leon.strauch@camunda.com

[3] https://camunda.com/blog/2020/08/from-project-to-program-establishing-a-center-of-excellence/

[4] https://www.forrester.com/report/techniker-krankenkasse-excels-with-customer-experience-through-process/RES180454

[5] https://camunda.com/state-of-process-orchestration/

[6] https://resources.fenergo.com/reports/kyc-trends-2023-report#main-content

[7] https://www.bls.gov/opub/mlr/2023/article/labor-force-and-macroeconomic-projections.htm#:~:text=BLS%20projects%20that%20the%20annual,from%20164.3%20million%20in%202022.

[8] https://www.economist.com/europe/2022/10/06/there-are-not-enough-germans-to-do-the-jobs-germany-needs

[9] https://securities.cib.bnpparibas/t1-settlement-ready/

[10] https://camunda.com/state-of-process-orchestration/

[11] https://camunda.com/process-orchestration/maturity/

[12] https://www.amazon.com/dp/1086302095

[13] https://page.camunda.com/wp-forrester-tei-study-2024

[14] https://docs.camunda.io/docs/components/concepts/workflow-patterns/

[15] https://camunda.com/blog/2022/07/why-process-orchestration-needs-advanced-workflow-patterns/

[16] https://www.researchgate.net/figure/IBM-System-Science-Institute-Relative-Cost-of-Fixing-Defects_fig1_255965523

[17] https://camunda.com/case-study/t-mobile-austria/

[18] https://camunda.com/platform/modeler/connectors/

[19] https://camunda.com/platform/tasklist/.

[20] https://camunda.com/blog/2022/03/why-goldman-sachs-built-a-brand-new-platform/

[21] https://camunda.com/blog/2018/07/camunda-days-nyc-goldman-sachs-workflow-platform/

[22] https://www.mckinsey.com/featured-insights/mckinsey-on-books/rewired

[23] https://en.wikipedia.org/wiki/PDCA

[24] https://www.noahpinion.blog/p/american-workers-need-lots-and-lots

[25] https://www.bain.com/insights/automations-ultimate-goal-the-augmented-workforce

[26] https://en.wikipedia.org/wiki/Crossing_the_Chasm

[27] https://www.bain.com/insights/intelligent-automation-getting-employees-embrace-bots/

[28] https://architectelevator.com

[29] https://itrevolution.com/product/accelerate/

[30] https://techbeacon.com/app-dev-testing/7-takeaways-accelerate-your-devops

[31] https://dora.dev/

[32] https://flowframework.org/ffc-project-to-product-book/

[33] https://mcfunley.com/choose-boring-technology

[34] https://teamtopologies.com/book

[35] https://teamtopologies.com/key-concepts

[36] https://teamtopologies.com/book

[37] https://engineering.atspotify.com/2020/08/how-we-use-golden-paths-to-solve-fragmentation-in-our-software-ecosystem/

[38] https://backstage.io/

[39] https://www.mckinsey.com/industries/technology-media-and-telecommunications/our-insights/unleashing-developers-full-talents-an-interview-with-twilios-ceo

[40] https://page.camunda.com/camundacon-2022-national-bank-of-canada

[41] https://camunda.com/process-orchestration/maturity/

[42] https://processautomationbook.com/

[43] https://camunda.com/state-of-process-automation-2020/

[44] https://camunda.com/wp-content/uploads/2023/01/WP-StateOfProcessOrchestration2023-FIN-en.pdf

[45] https://martinfowler.com/articles/talk-about-platforms.html

[46] https://doi.org/10.1016/j.indmarman.2020.03.017

[47] https://camunda.com/blog/2022/12/how-to-create-grow-center-of-excellence/#how-involved-should-khul

[48] https://landscape.cncf.io/

[49] https://www.mckinsey.com/capabilities/operations/our-insights/your-questions-about-automation-answered

[50] https://camunda.com/blog/2022/12/how-to-create-grow-center-of-excellence/

[51] https://blog.hubspot.com/service/lunch-and-learn

[52] https://www.camundacon.com/

[53] https://camunda.com/events/

[54] https://community.camunda.com/

[55] https://camunda.com/case-studies/

[56] https://academy.camunda.com/

[57] https://docs.camunda.io/docs/components/best-practices/best-practices-overview/

[58] https://camunda.com/blog/2022/02/whats-in-your-hyperautomation-tech-stack/

[59] https://blog.bernd-ruecker.com/process-automation-in-harmony-with-rpa-720effdb0513

[60] https://engineering.atspotify.com/2020/08/how-we-use-golden-paths-to-solve-fragmentation-in-our-software-ecosystem/

[61] https://page.camunda.com/camundacon-2023-provinzial

[62] https://page.camunda.com/camundacon-2023-natwest

[63] https://page.camunda.com/camundacon-2022-national-bank-of-canada

[64] https://page.camunda.com/camundacon-2023-provinzial

[65] https://page.camunda.com/camundacon-2022-desjardins

[66] https://camunda.com/blog/2022/03/why-goldman-sachs-built-a-brand-new-platform/

[67] https://page.camunda.com/ccs2022-client-use-cases-by-goldman-sachs

[68] https://page.camunda.com/camundacon-2023-city-of-munich

[69] https://page.camunda.com/de/process-automation-forum-live-dt

[70] https://docs.google.com/presentation/d/1fyVtpYAcGqdrLT5xeKCEeuLp3TsCLJzeVFI351xEulc/edit#slide=id.g29dceac4d0b_0_0

[71] https://hbr.org/2016/09/know-your-customers-jobs-to-be-done

[72] https://martinfowler.com/bliki/BoundedContext.html

[73] https://martinfowler.com/bliki/UbiquitousLanguage.html

[74] https://docs.camunda.io/docs/components/best-practices/development/service-integration-patterns/

[75] https://docs.camunda.io/docs/components/tasklist/introduction-to-tasklist/

[76] https://docs.camunda.io/docs/components/modeler/forms/camunda-forms-reference/

[77] https://bpmn.io/toolkit/form-js/

[78] https://camunda.com/platform/operate/

[79] https://camunda.com/platform/modeler/

[80] https://marketplace.camunda.com/

[81] https://www.oreilly.com/library/view/adopting-innersource/9781492041863/ch01.html

[82] https://docs.camunda.io/docs/components/best-practices/development/handling-data-in-processes/

[83] https://blog.bernd-ruecker.com/process-automation-in-harmony-with-rpa-720effdb0513

[84] https://camunda.com/platform/optimize/

[85] https://docs.camunda.io/docs/components/best-practices/operations/reporting-about-processes/#connecting-custom-business-intelligence-systems-bi-data-warehouses-dwh-or-monitoring-solutions

[86] https://docs.camunda.io/docs/components/best-practices/development/handling-data-in-processes/

[87] https://docs.camunda.io/docs/next/components/best-practices/development/testing-process-definitions/

[88] https://en.wikipedia.org/wiki/Infrastructure_as_code

[89] https://www.amazon.com/Team-Topologies-Organizing-Business-Technology/dp/B07VWYNGCQ/

[90] https://martinfowler.com/articles/talk-about-platforms.html

[91] https://engineering.atspotify.com/2020/08/how-we-use-golden-paths-to-solve-fragmentation-in-our-software-ecosystem/

[92] https://www.mckinsey.com/industries/technology-media-and-telecommunications/our-insights/unleashing-developers-full-talents-an-interview-with-twilios-ceo

[93] https://itrevolution.com/articles/run-your-platform-like-a-business-within-a-business/

[94] https://teamtopologies.com/videos-slides/what-is-platform-as-a-product-clues-from-team-topologies

[95] https://teamtopologies.com/book

[96] https://blog.bernd-ruecker.com/the-7-sins-of-workflow-b3641736bf5c

[97] https://www.amazon.com/-/en/Accelerate-Building-Performing-Technology-Organizations/dp/1942788339

[98] https://www.amazon.com/The-Phoenix-Project-audiobook/dp/B00VATFAMI/

[99] https://www.amazon.com/Project-Product-Survive-Disruption-Framework/dp/B07KCLW84N/

[100] https://docs.camunda.io/docs/components/best-practices/development/handling-data-in-processes/

[101] https://docs.camunda.io/docs/next/self-managed/about-self-managed/

[102] https://www.techtarget.com/searchcloudcomputing/definition/noisy-neighbor-cloud-computing-performance

[103] https://github.com/camunda/zeebe-process-test

[104] https://docs.camunda.io/docs/components/best-practices/architecture/sizing-your-environment/#sizing-your-runtime-environment

[105] https://camunda.com/blog/2022/06/how-to-achieve-geo-redundancy-with-zeebe/

[106] https://camunda.com/customer/nasa/

[107] https://page.camunda.com/cclive-2021-goldman-sachs

[108] https://blog.bernd-ruecker.com/how-to-benefit-from-robotic-process-automation-rpa-9edc04430afa

[109] https://www.oreilly.com/library/view/practical-process-automation/9781492061441/

[110] https://www.confluent.io/de-de/blog/data-streams-are-nothing-without-actionable-insights-leading-to-actions/

[111] https://www.oreilly.com/library/view/practical-process-automation/9781492061441/

[112] https://camunda.com/blog/2022/07/why-process-orchestration-needs-advanced-workflow-patterns/

[113] https://www.amazon.com/Real-Life-BPMN-4th-introduction-DMN/dp/1086302095

[114] https://docs.camunda.io/docs/components/best-practices/management/doing-a-proper-poc/

[115] https://github.com/camunda-community-hub/spring-zeebe/

[116] https://github.com/camunda-community-hub/zeebe-client-csharp

[117] https://docs.camunda.io/docs/components/best-practices/architecture/deciding-about-your-stack/

[118] https://docs.camunda.io/docs/components/best-practices/development/testing-process-definitions/

[119] https://docs.camunda.io/docs/next/components/modeler/web-modeler/new-web-modeler/

[120] https://camunda.com/download/modeler/

[121] https://github.com/camunda-community-hub/web-modeler-github-sync-example

[122] https://docs.camunda.io/docs/guides/devops-lifecycle/integrate-web-modeler-in-ci-cd/

[123] https://github.com/camunda/connectors/tree/main/connectors

[124] https://github.com/camunda/connectors/tree/main/bundle/default-bundle

[125] https://www.kotterinc.com/methodology/8-steps/

Printed in Great Britain
by Amazon